You're Not Moving Slow Enough

The Unexpected Formula to Lasting Influence

Ariel Halevi

Printed in Israel & USA

ISBN: 978-965-92575-0-8

For information regarding the author and the author's services, please contact: www.vayomar.com

To my love,
Heli Anna Halevi

Here's a FREE Gift for You!

Enjoy our *FAST START* Persuasion Checklist

In under 3 minutes, you'll discover…

- How to create lasting influence without needing to use authority, force, or fear.
- How to use a tool that is 10x more powerful than even the strongest intellectual arguments.
- How to avoid gratification traps™ and achieve lifelong impact.

Download our COMPLIMENTARY checklist at:

http://SlowEnough.com/guide

Table of contents

It All Starts with a Marshmallow

Little Robbie sat silently, his eyes glued to the object on the table in front of him—a single marshmallow. A tiny, unassuming ball of sugar. Robbie, with his blue wool sweater and mop of tousled brown hair, just happened to be the kind of kid that loved marshmallows. And yet, he sat there, fighting the growing urge to reach over and grab it. That's because, after he sat down by the table with the coveted marshmallow, he was given a choice: eat the marshmallow and savor the sweetness, OR wait until the person who brought him into the room returned, in which case—if he had not yet eaten the marshmallow—he would be rewarded with a second one for his patience. Then he'd have two.

That's the premise for one of my favorite experiments, conducted in Stanford in the late 1960's. Kids, around the age of five, were left alone in a room with a marshmallow. The test was simple—eat the initial marshmallow or wait and receive another one. The adult who brought them into the room told them the following: *"I am leaving the room now. The marshmallow is yours and you are free to eat it. But if, when I return, you have not eaten the marshmallow, I will give you a second one."* The children were then left alone for roughly 15 minutes.

It probably comes as no surprise that 66% of the children ended up buckling and eating the first marshmallow. But here's the kicker: Over 50 years down the road, the kids from the marshmallow test are still surveyed from time to time.

The results were astounding.

There is an overwhelming correlation between delayed gratification and the ability to succeed in life. Those that were able to put their immediate desires on hold were more successful later in life.

This famous marshmallow experiment inspired me to write this book about my experiences as a professional persuader. It made me realize that when it comes to trying to influence people around us and persuade them to think and act in a certain way, we are all just like those kids, sitting in front of tempting marshmallows. We face a similar choice between immediate action or waiting and holding out for a better outcome.

This is the core principle behind this book — *if you want to effectively persuade people, you need to understand when immediate gratification is holding you back.* This is critical, because for most of us—most of the time—our inability to persuade people is entirely our doing. And yet, that's also **great news** because it means it is almost entirely up to us to achieve the opposite outcome—effective persuasion. But first, we need to make sure to successfully arrive at a preliminary achievement: we need to get people to connect with *us* before we get them to connect the dots that make up the world as we see it.

The use of powerful tools, like well-structured arguments, killer facts, respectable sources, impeccable timing, and an overall impressive intellectual capacity are simply not effective when they do not have a solid interpersonal foundation to stand on. At best, you'll be shooting blank bullets; but even more likely (almost tragically), your efforts will prove counterproductive.

So, what is the solid interpersonal foundation I was referring to? Answer: It is the emotional experience others have when they interact with **you**.

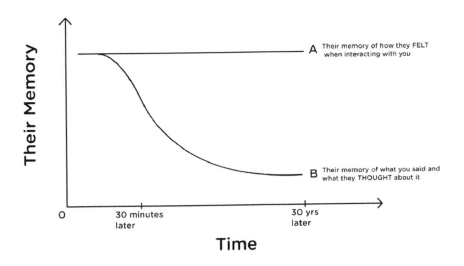

Cut to its simplest form, this graph shows the following: your ability to remember all the ins and outs and details of a prolonged debate is extremely limited and is going to taper off quickly. In fact, people will forget most of the things you said within just a few short minutes. However, how you *feel* about someone fades very slowly, sometimes not at all. If someone left a very positive or negative impression on you, you will maintain that impression for years to come.

Now try to recall a recent argument you had. How much time and energy did you spend on arguments and facts? How much energy did you invest in making others listen to what you had to say?

Did you make it so that others enjoyed hearing what you had to say, leaving them with a good taste in their mouths—you know, like a marshmallow—to remember the conversation by?

This is where delayed gratification comes out to play. Instead of focusing on the cognitive side of our interactions, such as being an excellent debater or having all the facts, we want to first put our focus on developing positive and pleasant interactions that are built on a foundation of emotional intelligence (EQ). Emotional intelligence, not intellectual intelligence, is what this book will show you how to develop and use in order to improve your persuasive capabilities. Pleasant interactions will lead to stronger relationships, which in turn will lead to more frequent interactions, creating a greater number of opportunities to influence. These relationships will be the key to your ability to be more persuasive and ultimately exercise true influence.

So how is it done?

In order to turn ourselves into the kind of person that practices and thrives through delayed gratification when trying to persuade, we need to learn to avoid three gratification traps.

1. Our false sense of urgency
2. Our need for absolute certainty
3. Our need for credit

Fair warning—these traps are *really clever*. If at any point, you find yourself staring in horror at the page in front of you, with a crushing realization that you have fallen into one (or all) of these traps on a daily basis, it's ok! You are not alone. The good news is that learning to avoid these traps is possible, and this book is precisely about that.

After we learn all about these dangerous gratification traps and how to identify them early on in conversations, we will then learn how to successfully avoid them by using a five-step process that ensures we will *never* fall into them again. Well… "never" is a big word. Given that I still find myself at the bottom of these traps sometimes, let's just say that, together, we will learn how to dramatically reduce the number of times we do fall. In turn, this will dramatically increase the number of times we get that second marshmallow as people respond to us with a smile, and as they say those beautiful words: "*You know, I haven't thought of it that way… interesting!*"

Choose Your Own Path

This is a book using delayed gratification to increase our ability to persuade people. We want what we want, and we want it when we want it, which is usually "now!" Not to mention that waiting often goes against what society is relentlessly teaching us…

- *"The time is now!"*
- *"Hurry up!"*
- *"This deal won't last long!"*
- *"Have it on my desk first thing in the morning!"*

Put frankly, delayed gratification is not likely to be our strong suit, and that is 100% alright. After all, that marshmallow can be exceptionally tempting!

So here's the deal—the first chapter provides a foundation for all of the sexy tips and tricks to follow. But they don't hold that action-packed punch you might be craving, now that you've taken a proactive step and are reading these words. Are they stuffed with good content?

You bet.

Are they worth reading?

Absolutely.

But if you're low on patience and don't feel like reading through all these pages before you get to the 'meat'—that's fine.

I get it. After all, I'm not going to expect you to delay gratification at this point. You still haven't read the book.

Go ahead and skip to chapter 2 if you can't be bothered right now with theoretical foundations. When you're done, you're welcome to come back and read this part. After all, this is your book.

For those of you who want a little background for the tips and tools I present in this book, the next 23 pages will give you just that. They offer a broader context to the field I have come to love and have dedicated my life to over the past 15 years.

Let's get started!

| Chapter 1 |

2%

What is persuasion?

Most people see the ability to persuade as something that a select few are born with. They see influential people that can easily convince others to come over to their side, and they chalk it up to natural predisposition. "The gift of the gab" is one of the phrases that indicates this thinking. Another is "charming" (from the word "charisma," which literally means "Gift of the Gods" in ancient Greek).

I am here to tell you, that simply is not true! Instead, **persuasion is a skill**, above all else. The ability to manage the <u>process</u> of leading a person to the adoption of a belief and related behavior(s) **can be acquired**. You don't need to be gifted. You do, however, need to be educated in *how to be persuasive*, which is what this book is about and you will need to practice. A lot. That part is up to you. Just as becoming a persuasive person is entirely *up to you*.

Yes, some may start from a more favorable position. After all, talent does exist. But if I have learned and experienced one truth over the years, it is this: everyone and anyone—with enough practice and drive—can become an effective persuader and a powerful communicator. Practicing the art of persuasion daily causes it to eventually become second nature—a powerful habit.

It is important to note, that I am not saying **that** before you know it, you can expect to hold the same levels of charisma, God-given charm, and mesmerizing eloquence as those that are capable of drawing crowds by the thousands. This level of persuasion may not be in your specific reach. But the reality is this overwhelming level of ability is not necessary for everyone.

Most people don't need to draw and mesmerize mega audiences. For the majority of us, success means getting more leeway from our bosses; increasing our sales by dozens of percentiles; dramatically reducing tensions with our spouses and other loved ones; and drawing in hundreds of people—perhaps thousands—over a period of our lifetime to support a political stance or a long-held belief. Now *that* is definitely within your grasp. I don't need to know you in order to fully stand behind this promise. It's not about eclipsing the "greats," it's about being the very best you have it in you to be. My passion has never been to create rock stars. It is simply to help as many people as possible realize their full potential, using interpersonal communication and persuasion skills to progress towards the success they want.

What persuasion is NOT: *A complex, completely over-your-head art form that you need a PhD to comprehend*

While we might come across phrases in this book like "cross-cultural barriers", "non-verbal communication", "rational and non-rational decision making", "mediation," "conflict resolution", and a litany of other professional lingo attached to persuasion, those are just characteristics of persuasion. Different angles of persuasion if you will. As we defined it just a moment ago, persuasion is—and will always be—the process of taking someone <u>willingly</u> from point A to point B. That's all it is.

What do I get from becoming a powerful persuader?

Your relationships will grow deeper and more fulfilling; your confidence will propel you to new heights; and you will become a more well-rounded person. You'll see a steep drop in any tendencies you might have to say things you shouldn't say. As a whole, you will make far fewer mistakes in your professional relationships. Executive managers in your company will start noticing you more. You will appear to have developed an "Executive Presence" and can expect shorter promotion cycles. You will have more soft power—the kind that no "boss" can take away from you.

Persuasion puts you in the driver's seat.

Think of the many incredible people that we consider successful. More than likely, you can quickly pinpoint their ability to persuade others. From great speakers to business people, persuasion allows you to sell your reality to the rest of the world. So, what do you get from becoming a powerful persuader? You give yourself the open door to achieve newly-imagined levels of success.

I could go on for days about the levels of success you can find along the way, but one of the most important aspects of this success will be the strengthening and deepening of your relationships: personal and professional. When you can learn to effectively communicate and make your way of thinking more attractive and reasonable to others, something wonderful will happen. You will start to notice that these relationships are generally and steadily more pleasant.

Conversations will flow smoother and you will see a steady decreasing of stress in your life. Getting things done will take less effort and be more enjoyable.

But why move slower? Isn't faster better?

Working *faster* does not equate to working *better*. In fact, when it comes to persuasion, the opposite is more frequently true. You can lead a horse to water, but you can't make it drink. In the same vein, we can shout until our lungs are pleading for a rest, but it will not bring others over to our side. Instead, we can learn to take the steady approach and make sure they are thirsty first. If we carefully walk them around in the hot sun (in our case, a carefully constructed conversation designed to make our point of view infinitely attractive), they will arrive at our way of thinking without being forced to do so. And when that happens, influence is permanent… **lasting**.

One of the greatest benefits that comes from this approach is that of lasting impact. If we have brought someone to our line of thinking for a specific topic without dragging them kicking and screaming, we have created a situation where we are a person who provides the comfort of certainty, not the pain of uncertainly and reluctant change. Ultimately, this is a trust building dynamic. This trust carries over into all other conversations, spanning many other topics.

- Move fast for instant gratification.
- Move slow for lasting impact.

When you achieve lasting impact, there's another important benefit waiting for you.

Short Term Impact Requires Constant Investment

For much of our time on this planet, different forms of authority have driven our world. From brute force to financial incentives, raw power has often been the best route to success.

The harsh truth is that brute force can *definitely* get you what you want. Paying someone to do what you ask is not only the basis of our economy, but a tacit form of interaction in today's world. The threat of termination is enough to scare people back **into line**, but what effects does it have **down the line**?

While it might sound appealing to get immediate compliance—a nice juicy marshmallow if you will—it is not sustainable.

Two negative outcomes are likely to await you:

(1) Eventually there will be a breaking point, with threats of termination causing an individual to find new employment; physical dominance resulting in allied resistance, or enough funds will be generated that your "bribes" will no longer be sufficient.

(2) Even if you don't reach that breaking point, without constant reinforcement—which is quite taxing on your resources—your impact will diminish almost instantly.

With all of this having been said, I don't want to push the idea that persuasion—or influence without authority—is the be-all and end-all for getting people to behave in a certain way. Not at all.

Not all interpersonal relationships and processes need to be persuasion based, as every rule has its exceptions. Sometimes, short-term results are the main priority. Depending on the situation, an immediate need can take priority over long-term influence.

Put simply, sometimes we don't *need* lasting impact. In these situations, calling on one's formal authority when demanding a certain behavior or action is the right way to go, even if the other person doesn't understand why it's being demanded or doesn't happen to agree with it.

However, there seems to be broad misperception around how many situations call for this approach. **"Gratification traps,"** which we will look at later in this book, make it seem like 98% of the disagreements we get into call for a strong-arm approach. In reality, instances like these account for approximately 2% of the time, maybe even less.

---

*Remember, justifiable use of force or authority is an **exception** to the rule, and should be treated as such.*

We live in a highly-structured world, which has clear and established hierarchies set in place. The very nature of hierarchies draws us to an authority-based predisposition towards influence. This means that persuasion, especially persuasion revolving around delayed gratification, is not likely to be our natural response.

This innate predisposition towards persuasion is further reinforced by the ever-growing speed in which the world is moving, which is combined with a constant overflow of information. Everyone is under increasing pressure and this pressure needs relief—fast!

A fast-moving business world can push this urgency to even higher levels. If you have ever felt this pressure creeping in, then I am sure you can relate with an endless supply of your own examples.

*"The marketing budget **needs** approval today."*

*"I **only have** 3 days to hit my sales quota."*

*"My **make-or-break** presentation is on Friday."*

It doesn't matter if we are persuading a colleague, customer, or spouse, because we have been taught to see **everything** as urgent. We may very well be the most impatient generation in of all human history.

Vicious Cycle

"But Ariel, you don't understand, I can't afford to adopt these long-term methodologies right now. If I don't meet my targets THIS WEEK, there is no 'long term' for me here anyway!"

I can't tell you how many times I have heard this line of reasoning in my years as a consultant—especially as a consultant to large corporations. The unfortunate byproduct of this widely prevailing approach is a vicious cycle—I don't have time to convince them, so I force them! If the people I force into a given behavior don't truly believe in what I am saying (or see the light after the fact), and if they are antagonized by being treated that way, then we will be required to continue overseeing them to reinforce their desired conduct; this places a massive drain on our resources. Without enough resources, we can't adopt longer paths to influence, and the cycle starts again.

In *Steven Covey's 7 Habits for Highly Effective People*, his four-quadrant box clearly demonstrates the benefits and time savings of allocating resources to box Q-2, where things are "Important" and "Not Urgent". As a professional persuader, I can vouch for the benefits. The more time you take up front, the less is required later.

True persuasion is permanent, and works like an asset that yields compounded interest over time; it keeps working for you and makes you grow your influence steadily. By taking a moment to breath and slowing your pace, the negative behavioral byproducts of your time-sensitive rationale will gradually evaporate. The sooner you start moving slower, the faster and more powerful your impact.

	Urgent	Non-Urgent
Important	**Q-1: Quadrant of Necessity** • Impending deadlines (that are important and have long-term consequence to your life) • Crises/Emergencies • Resolving immediate problems • Certain e-mails that may change your life (e.g., job app, biz opport)	**Q-2: Quadrant of Quality and Personal Leadership** • Building long-term solutions/systems • Relationship building • Building your dream career/business • Personal/Skill development • Improving your health/wellness • Finding your life partner
Not Important	**Q-3: Quadrant of Deception** • Interruptions/Distractions • Most phone calls/e-mails • Attending inconsequential meetings • Spending a lot of time on a task (report, e-mail) that has little to no impact to your goals/life in long run • Dealing with others' requests	**Q-4: Quadrant of Waste** • Mindless TV/web surfing / chatting • Reading gossip sites/forums • Watching/reading news (to an extent) • Certain phone calls/e-mails • Excessive gaming • Idling • Any time wasting activity

Slow Is Not Really Slower

The strategies in this book may seem painfully slow at first. Our hyperactive society has drilled into our heads that anything not moving at the speed of light is painfully dragging on. This is simply not the case in persuasive dynamics. Instead, we should think of the word "slow" as more similar to "thorough" or "self-sustainable." A well-constructed effort is going to outgun sprints that leave us (and others!) winded too early in the race. The better we get at moving slower, the faster we will be able to persuade people to come over to our side and stay there for the near and foreseeable future. Remember, Rome wasn't built in a day, but thousands of years later, it still stands magnificent.

For persuasive impact to have meaning and stand the test of time, there are two necessary understandings:

1. The person we are trying to influence genuinely enjoyed our presence and wants to be around us more.
2. The person we are trying to influence genuinely wants to adopt our point of view and accept the behavioral changes.

By having these two prerequisites in place, we open the door to limitless possibilities, not only with this person but also with the people they in turn have influence over. Sticking tight to these principles allows the people we interact with to walk away with an inner drive. This drive will sustain their newfound resolve long after our interaction with them, even providing influence when we are no longer near them. This ensures that our energy drives are not drained dry by a need to constantly stay in contact with the people we wish to persuade and maintain their resolve in our favor.

For all of you selling something (whether ideas or products), here is something to look forward to—by subscribing to this understanding, you open yourself up to a world of opportunities that are significantly more cost-effective than the world, which relies heavily on money, authority, or force as tools of persuasion.

This value will come full swing when you think about the "millennial" generation. This generation, born in the early 1980s, respects its own autonomy and judgment and simply does not respond to authority in a traditional manner. If you have any desires or hopes of learning how to work with this new generation (as a manager or a colleague), your best bet is to learn how to influence without authority.

External Pressure vs. Inner Drive

Cultivating a steady inner drive goes hand-in-hand with steady persuasion. In many cases, a person's contrary point of view is like a rubber band. As we apply greater amounts of force, we are essentially stretching the rubber band to its limit; it will stay in place only as long as we continue to apply pressure. But, when we release the rubber band, it instantly snaps back into place, often damaging us in the process. In fact, the more pressure we put on it, the faster and harder it shoots back our way.

This is usually the outcome when you bully, force, or intimidate someone into action. In fact, the most likely outcome of any of these "fast and easy" approaches is the elimination of true inner drive, and worse still, the creation and fueling of an opposing drive. In such cases, not only will the other person not stay the course once we are no longer there to apply these various pressures, but they will even rebound in the opposite direction, leading them to avoid future interactions with us. This is why it is so important for them to *want* to engage with us. Once we have helped establish their inner drive in a way that's aligned with our way of thinking, it will keep them sustained as they move forward well after we have stepped away.

> *"A man convinced against his will,*
> *is of the same opinion, still"*
>
> -Samuel Butler
> 17th Century Poet

When we establish a real, proper inner drive in the other person (and when we do it in a pleasant way) not only will they not "snap back" into their original thoughts and behaviors, but we will also benefit from an important byproduct: a better relationship with them. This relationship will serve as an important foundation for future interactions that call for persuasion.

Freight-Train Jill
A.K.A. Are you that person?

I met Jill and I thought to myself that I had always known her. I think all of us have known Jill at some point or another. Either that, or someone just like her. She was wildly outspoken and everyone knew all of her opinions.

Why?

Because she shouted them from the rooftops. According to Jill, you either didn't care enough about the big issues; you cared too much about the small ones; or you simply failed to speak your mind and engage in verbal combat. Needless to say, it could be frustrating, tiring, and downright grating to be around her.

So "freight-train" Jill continued on, challenging everyone she came across. It was almost as if she NEEDED confrontation. Then she met Ken, a soft-spoken sort. Ken is the kind of person who makes the entire world slow down. Despite his calm disposition, it turns out that Ken was just one *"you are exactly what is wrong with society"* away from snapping.

I was throwing a dinner party and both Ken and Jill were there. Ken had voiced his uncertainty about the validity of a recent political survey when Jill jumped in, cutting him off in mid-sentence.

"You don't know what you are talking about!"

This was classic Jill, enforcing her will, her certainties, and it made everyone at the table uncomfortable.

"Why is that?" Ken was approaching her reckless comment with his usual calm resolve.

She listed not one, not two, but five reasons why she thought Ken was so far off base. From "a clear lack of empathy" to "learn to check your sources," you could see Ken growing tauter with each self-righteous exclamation. She was stretching the rubber band, ignoring just how tight it was getting.

Remarkably, it did not snap. Not during the conversation at least. Ken offered some calm rebuttals. He carried on for two or three more exchanges, and then he simply ended it with a brief nod of his head and a "hmmm... I see your point." Jill was content. But I knew she had not only failed to reach him, she had lost him.

It was clear that this would be the last time Ken would bother to engage in any meaningful conversation with Jill. He simply let her have the last word and let the conversation die out.

The sad part is that she had not only failed in getting Ken to see her point of view on this topic—some of which may have been completely valid—but she had lost any chance of persuading him on other topics in *future* interactions.

Finally, she had also sacrificed this potential with several other people at the party—people who thought differently than she did, but had no desire to suffer the pain of debating with her.

TAKEAWAY: Make sure your passion doesn't come across as bullying. Chances are that Jill wasn't trying to be a bully. No doubt she just thought she was being assertive and knowledgeable. Likely, she thought she was being passionate. Passion inspires, Jill didn't. Bullied persuasion leads to resentment. Both outcomes will outlive the specific conversation that led to them.

What <u>you said</u> vs. how <u>they felt</u>

People remember how they felt when they engaged with you more intensely and for a much longer time than they do what you said and what they thought about it. This means that for future conversations, discussions, and "persuasion-heavy" incidents, having an already established feeling of good-will can be worth its weight in gold.

It boils down to a simple Persuasion Equation

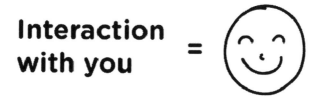

The not-so-dirty secret about persuasion is that how people feel when they think of you often dictates your overall ability to persuade them. This is regardless of the specific topic being discussed or the given circumstances surrounding any given conversation.

Well-reasoned words are not always enough—certainly not at first. And, for developing truly substantial relationships, taking into consideration how we make others feel is not just recommended, it's absolutely critical.

All the important elements of persuasion rest on a basic, fundamentally important, interpersonal foundation—the experience you create for the person you are trying to persuade will have a major impact on the outcome.

Even the most compelling of arguments and business values are likely to fall on deaf ears when received from a person whose opinion of us comes from a negative experience.

When that foundation is solid, everything flows more easily, and we can even get away with lower-quality arguments, facts, and in the world of business competitive differentiations. Create a great experience **and** use top-quality arguments, facts, and impressive sources, and you can move heaven and earth.

Like it or not, human beings are not robots. Most of us are often driven by non-rational, decision-making processes. We do not have the capacity to operate in a way that is purely rational. In fact, as the world grows more complex—moving faster and gaining information at exponential rates never seen before—we move even *further* away from rational decision-making processes!

The bevy of available information and our strong need to avoid uncertainty leads us to seek—sometimes desperately—safe havens or comfort zones. We turn to close friends for advice, even on topics they might know little about. We do this, because we know and trust them. Trust can't be bought or forced; it is 100% earned. This is as true with leaders of nations as it is with people like you and me. We gravitate to people that we enjoy working with and being around while we push away those who are unpleasant. We do so even if they have more functional benefits to offer us. Good or bad, it's basic human behavior.

Chapter 2

EQ Before IQ

If you want to build a ship, don't drum up people together to collect wood and don't assign them tasks and work, but rather teach them to long for the endless immensity of the sea.

- Antoine de Saint-Exupery

Making someone do something through brute force—as we looked at in the last chapter—rarely leaves a lasting positive impression. Instead, it often encourages a setting where more force and energy are required each time to get the same results. If you have ever worked in a team environment, you have likely seen this happen, or even experienced it yourself.

Managers that demand respect are often the very same ones who try to have their hand in every project. Beyond the toll that this micro-managing dynamic takes on their energy, it inevitably brings about lower-quality results as their team only does the very minimum required to get their boss off their backs (not to mention the inevitable decay in authority as force is applied over and over again).

But this dynamic doesn't have to be limited to managers in organizations. Think about conversations with people you are doing business with (your construction manager who under-delivered, the salesperson who sold you a bad couch, or someone you're talking to about buying their car). These are all situations where it's easy to succumb to the temptation of "authority." We often end up thinking, "Hey, I am the client here," which—in other words—translates to "I am the boss."

Defaulting to this way of thinking is incredibly easy to do. Even after all the years I've spent studying and implementing the science of persuasion and practicing it intensively (I own a company with dozens of employees), I still have times when I just want to say "Screw it!" and take the "fast" route. But then I remind myself that the "fast route" doesn't lead to lasting results, and rarely gets me there faster.

Much like the quote at the start of this chapter, accomplishing a project of any size can be done two ways: you can either tell someone to do something, or you can facilitate their desire to want to do it. The second option leads to far better results.

When you are dealing with people that you have an ongoing relationship with, and when the stakes are high, go even slower still. Not reaching in and taking the marshmallow is going to be tough, as your instinct is going to be one of haste ("I **need** this now!"). Even though it isn't always easy, wait for the second marshmallow and the lasting impact.

The four milestones of lasting persuasion are:

1. Getting them to ***want* to listen** to us.
2. Getting them to ***want* to agree** with us.
3. Getting them to ***adopt*** our point of view.
4. Getting them to **behave** accordingly.

With the amount of haste in our world, the need for things to happen *right now* leads to an overall sense of uncertainty, and that creates quite a bit of discomfort. Our strong need to avoid uncertainty leads to us to seek—sometimes desperately—safe havens. We pine for our own little forts of certainty. We turn to close friends for advice, even on topics about which they have little knowledge. Why? Because we know and trust them. They are within our comfort zone. We gravitate to people we enjoy being around while we move away from those who are unpleasant, even if they have more functional benefits to offer us and can be instrumental to achieving our goals.

While there are plenty of experts out there, what do I really know about them? Can I trust them to have my back like the people I have known and worked with for years?

Here's the thing about us humans, we tend to procrastinate. We have a natural tendency to avoid or delay doing the things we don't want to do to, even when they really need to get done. On the flip side, we quite understandably seek out the things that bring us pleasure—things we are good at. We equally seek to engage with people whom we trust and feel comfortable being around.

"So Ariel, how is this helpful to me?"

In order to persuade others and bring them around to your way of thinking, you need to establish yourself as someone they are comfortable with. You need to come off in a way that is worthy of trust. You need to make them *feel* that your words are worth listening to. Once that happens, you will have put in place the most important prerequisite to persuasion. The value will be greater than simply increasing your chances of persuading them right here and now. You will also have laid the foundation of a relationship that can outlive the context of this specific conversation. This relationship will support you in future conversations, reaching out to include topics that may justify your persuasion efforts.

Once comfort and trust have been established, expertise can and should kick in.

Combine both well, and you will become unstoppable!

What gut feeling are you creating?

When people meet you, they have an almost instinctive gut response: their reaction is either positive or negative.

If their response is negative, you are tagged as a "burden" and they will consciously or unconsciously push you away.

This comes back to the comfort zone behavior. You being tagged as a burden will manifest in them answering other people's emails first, delaying meetings with you, forgetting to follow up with you, etc. Many times, they may not even be aware that they are doing these things. From my experience, most people aren't aware of the boundaries of their own comfort zone or of how it's affecting their daily routines.

Bottom line: if we find ourselves outside of their comfort zone, we will find it very hard to engage with them, let alone persuade them of anything. This is true even when we have value to offer them.

Our being tagged as a burden could be the result of any number of reasons, some well-founded: an unpleasant attitude, a negative past experience they had with us, a perception that we are a competitive threat, the tone of our voice, or even our body odor. Other reasons may be completely random: we remind them of someone they don't like, we fall under one of their negative stereotypes, or maybe we just happen to be friends with someone they don't like. The fact that we had little or nothing to do with these examples doesn't spare us the fallout. If this happens, we simply need to accept that we are starting at a disadvantage. We need to work even harder to replace the initial negative experience they had with us with as many positive ones as necessary to gain access to their comfort zone.

If, on the other hand, their response is positive, then we are tagged as "assets" and can expect the exact opposite behavior. The more intense their positive gut-response to us, the closer we are to the center of their comfort zone, and the more they will gravitate towards us.

Imagine the right-most part of the above negative/positive axis as being positioned perfectly in the center of their comfort zone.

The key to becoming a valuable asset is to ensure that their interactions with you are generally pleasant.

This does not mean that we can't say "no" from time to time. It doesn't mean we can't argue, even rigorously. Being pleasant is not the same as appeasing. There is a dramatic difference between trying to ensure a positive and pleasant dynamic and conceding to everything someone else wants. It's not so much about what you say as it is about how well you listen to what they say and *how* you say what you say. Just as important, it's about **when** you say what you say.

All in all, a person's experiential memory will be the sum of all of their experiences with you. Leaving a good first impression is always important as it gives them reason to want more interactions. Nevertheless, in many cases, if there is an irrational reason to why they don't like you off the bat, it doesn't necessarily mean you are doomed with them. If you wish to enhance your overall ability to influence people, focus on making the sum of your experiences positive. If you had a bad first experience, make the effort to create second and third encounters that leave a positive taste in their mouths. The more positive the sum of your encounters with them, the more enduring your relationship with them will be, regardless of occasional negative interactions and missteps.

I'm going to bring up the following equation as many times as necessary to cement its importance. If you want to be an effective persuader, finding success in all of your relationships, eat, breathe, and sleep this equation:

$$\textbf{Interaction with you} = \smiley$$

Your path to this equation will initially have almost nothing to do with your IQ or intellect. Not only that, but it also won't mainly depend on how educated you are or how well you construct your arguments.

That's right!

Your ability to persuade—through effective emotional intelligence—will rely heavily on your ability to provide the other person with as many "gratification moments." Often this will come at the expense of your own immediate gratification. They get instant gratification when conversing with you and you get a chance at lasting impact.

How effective you are as a persuader will be a factor of your choices between instant gratification (taking the marshmallow right away) and lasting impact on the person you are trying to persuade (letting them take the marshmallow and waiting for the second one).

When it comes to persuasion and influence without authority, the "marshmallow test" is represented by the following choice we shared earlier:

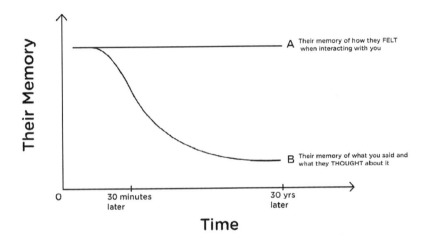

Making the right choice, deciding to make yourself an asset—not a burden—for others, will require overcoming two challenges: **awareness** and **control**. This is what EQ boils down to.

Awareness: the ability to identify the cause and effect relationship between things that happen and the emotions they trigger in you (as well as in the person you're trying to persuade). It is quite common to be unaware of the emotional impact certain stimuli have on us.

For instance:

Your last meeting of the week is with an important client. It's been a *tough* week, and you've been anxiously anticipating this meeting. Unfortunately, the meeting goes poorly. To make matters worse, you arrive home tired and frustrated, only to find a kitchen sink piled high with dishes. Your husband greets you with a smile and a kiss, but you respond angrily.

You: "*Why do I have to come home to this? We agreed that I will walk the dogs and handle the laundry while you go grocery shopping and wash the dishes!*"

Him: "*Hello to you too, dear. Rough day at the office?*"

You: [*Raising your voice*] "*DON'T GIVE ME THAT. THIS HAS NOTHING TO DO WITH ME HAVING A BAD DAY AND YOU KNOW IT! THIS IS ABOUT ME NOT HAVING TO COME HOME TO THIS MESS!*"

Now… here's the real question: are you really responding to the sink full of dirty dishes? Sure, that was the trigger, but was it the source of your response?

Is the intensity of your response proportionate to the frustration caused by a sink full of dirty dishes? You and your spouse both know that you've come home to dirty dishes before and did not respond this way. Sure, you were annoyed and said so in the past. Only this time, you're emotionally worn out from a long week, the built up stress from anticipating this important meeting, and the grave disappointment at the end of it.

Avoiding these kinds of dynamics will be almost impossible without an ability to link our emotional responses to the events that cultivate them and the triggers that unleash harsh and disproportionate responses. The faster we can do so in the wake of a destabilizing incident, the less likely we are to misplace frustrations and leave a bloody trail of "collateral damage."

Control: the ability to alter your behavior **after** correctly identifying the link between a stimulus and the emotional response it provoked. Being able to do this offers protection from disproportionate responses to other, smaller negative stimuli (like a piled up sink) that can serve as triggers.

Let's go back to the argument with your spouse. At some point, a voice in your head said, "What are you doing? Why are you screaming at him? You know it's not the dishes you're angry about, it's the disappointing meeting you just had."

We've all heard this voice of reason at some point during a shouting match or in the middle of an escalating argument. We've all found ourselves climbing up that tree, knowing full well that we're overreacting. And yet, so many times we ignore it. We brush aside this voice of reason and carry on, yelling even louder, further escalating the argument. We keep climbing that damn tree even though we know we're seconds away from saying something that we're going to regret. We can't help it.

This is what control is all about. It's about "helping it" even when all we want to do is let go of our filters. It's about listening to, not just hearing, our inner voice of reason (awareness) and stopping in our tracks. Control is about de-escalating the interaction and getting it back to trending in a more reasonable and productive direction.

It's anything but easy, I know. I've been there and have ignored that inner voice far too many times. I had always scored high on the Awareness part of EQ, but when it came to the control part of it, at times it was unbearable. Control has a lot to do with our temper, and adjusting temper can be very hard to do. **But it is possible.** It's a skill like any other; the hotter your temper, the harder you'll need to work to control it. **Awareness helps significantly and practice seals the deal.**

The faster we're able to alter, or even completely reverse, our misplaced responses and overall behavior, the greater our ability to be effective persuaders.

Going for lasting impact will require the ability to reach high levels of awareness, asking you to identify the link between stimuli and your emotional response in real time. Then, you can consciously change how you respond in spite of whatever painful or negative emotions you feel in the moment.

Our emotional intelligence determines our steady and consistent ability to delay our own gratification throughout the persuasion process. At the same time, it gives us the ability to grant the other person as many instant gratification moments as possible. The more we give them, the more they will enjoy interacting with us and the stronger their positive experiential memory of us will be. Achieve that, and you will have laid the most important foundation of any effort you make to persuade them, regardless of the topic at hand.

Five Seconds from Losing Control

Dunking her tea bag repeatedly into her mug, Anna looked over at Kylie and shook her head. *"Wow! When was the last time we saw each other?"* The quiet hum of the coffee shop matched the mood to a T; it was a perfect place to see an old friend.

Kylie sipped at her coffee, the raw sugar giving it a certain sweetness. *"Way too long. I can't believe it's almost been two years since Jake's house-warming party."*

"I've been following you on Facebook," Anna said smiling, "You've been busy!"

"Yeah, a lot has changed in my life over the past two years. A few months after the party, I started volunteering at the local shelter and helping out at the daycare by my apartment on weekends. Then I got promoted... it's been good!" Kylie tapped her knuckles on the right corner of the table. "I'm pretty sure it has to do with a new diet I started; it completely changed my energy levels. I started sleeping better, getting more done, and I'm happy. But enough about me, tell me about you... how have you been!?"

"What's the new diet?" Anna raised her eyebrow, signaling her curiosity while completely ignoring Kylie's question.

"Somebody at Jake's party talked my ear off about trying out a paleo diet and I looked into it. A few weeks after I started, I noticed that I felt incredible. I can't believe it took me so long to find a diet that feels like it was made for me!"

Anna's tea bag hung in the air, and she gave Kylie a disappointed look. "So you still eat meat..."

Kylie nodded matter-of-factly.

"Don't you care about the animals? Have you seen what they go through? Do you have any idea how the meat industry processes them?" Anna's voice rose with each question.

Kylie was moving uncomfortably in her seat. Her face no longer held the high-energy smile it had just moments ago. Anna didn't notice. She went on: "I have been a vegan for almost eight years now and still can't fathom how people can be so adamant about liberal rights and the importance of empathy between people, but then avert their eyes when it comes to living, breathing creatures and how they are mercilessly butchered on a regular basis."

"Well, I—"

Anna cut Kylie off. "You can get all of the same health benefits from going vegan. Not only do you show that you care about living things, but you will feel so good with your new lifestyle! You don't have all of that animal flesh rotting in your stomach and you avoid all of the carcinogens in animal products. So you spend a little more money and give up some places you may be used to going to. Big deal. At least you won't have murder weighing on your conscience. And, if we take it one step further, you also have a new appreciation for all of the life around you! Going vegan gives you a whole new sense of empathy. Really, veganism provides all of the value without any of the side effects."

Anna fell back into her chair. She was speaking so passionately that she hadn't noticed that she was practically on the edge of her seat, her face leaning over the table, right in front of Kylie's.

"I understand where you're coming from, Anna. I have some friends at work who are vegan and we have spoken about it quite a bit. I get it. I even joined the 'Meatless Monday' program to show my support. But if I stop this diet, I will most likely fall back into the low-energy patterns from before. I hated that. I'm actually helping people now! The volunteer work I do is important to me. Not only that, but I think it's important to the people I work with and support."

As she ended her last sentence, Kylie waited for Anna's acknowledgement. She was sure Anna would understand. Maybe she would even ask her about the nature of her work with the shelter. Or at least about the promotion she had gotten.

It didn't happen.

After another 25 minutes of insistence on the matter, Anna finally relented. She finally moved on to other topics, but the atmosphere had changed and they both felt slightly uncomfortable. Anna struggled to defuse her anger and disappointment with Kylie, and Kylie was offended. After skipping dessert and having paid the check, Kylie indicated that she was heading in the opposite direction (it wasn't true) and they said their goodbyes.

TAKEAWAY: No matter how passionate you are about something; effective persuasion should never be about you or the topic at hand. It's about always about **them** and what **they** care about. Anna's passion and single-mindedness blinded her to what Kylie held dear. She had disregarded Kylie's positive attributes and values and proceeded to associate her with murder. Nothing could be more counterproductive to her cause.

Anna is clearly a good person: she cares about animals and is committed to making the world a better place, even through personal sacrifice. But her remarkable capacity for empathy for animals was equaled by a remarkable lack of empathy for Kylie's needs and aspirations. After all, Kylie is a good person too. She has been volunteering to help those in need in her community despite how busy she has been, certainly more so since her promotion. Passion tends to make us look at the world in a binary way—black and white, right and wrong. Like it or not, both the world and people are too complex for such simple categorizations. What Anna didn't realize is that, by completely foregoing Kylie's positive behavior and values, and by showing little-to-no interest in the things Kylie chose to share at the start of their conversation, she had put her own values (not eating meat) over Kylie's (being happy and volunteering). In doing so, she created a situation where Kylie can't help but feel uncomfortable, judged, and spoken down to. Who wants feel like that? Who wants to be around people who make you feel like they are not enough? Anna did little to promote her cause and certainly failed to promote the chances of Kylie meeting her again in the next two years. What a waste.

| Chapter 3 |

Marshmallows Everywhere!

I have been dealing with persuasion for as long as I can remember. As a kid, I would go around looking for a good argument. Later on, after discovering the wonderful game of debating in college, I began my professional career in persuasion.

It was only years down this path that I had a revelation about the secret to <u>lasting impact</u> through persuasion.

As a competitive debater, I had been taught the power of a good argument and the importance of being able to back up any logical reasoning with the proper facts. I was also taught the importance of a strong stage presence and of confidence. As a competitive debater, you have to know how to shine on stage. It's all about *you* and the name of the game is winning. It is your job to go out and ensure that the other team—representing an opposing point of view—has no ground to stand on. You can only win if they lose. In Game Theory, this type of game is called "zero sum."

In truth, these were truly important teachings that helped me develop a razor-sharp way of thinking. They also helped my debating partner and I win some major international trophies. I loved it!

But, it wasn't until years later that I realized—in my very own "eureka!" moment—that these skills played a secondary role to the real source of deep and lasting persuasive impact.

As we saw in the last chapter—dealing with emotional intelligence—our ability to influence other people is executed through a four-step process, in which we encourage them to:

1. *Want* to listen to us.
2. *Want* to agree with us.
3. *Willingly* adopt our point of view.
4. *Willingly* behave accordingly.

The most important words in these four steps, and the words that define the entire point of this type of persuasion, are *"**want**"* and *"**willingly.**"*

It's not about us winning, and most certainly not about the people we interact with losing or feeling defeated. And, above all, it's not about us. It's about them.

Yes, it is our passion and commitment to an ideal or initiative that drive us to try and persuade others. But as soon as that passion leads us to them, the interpersonal interaction has to be all about the person we are trying to influence. This is the key to our chances of having a <u>lasting</u> impact on them.

Our ideas and beliefs are what drive us to interact with others, but then they need to be put aside for a while as we focus on building a productive interpersonal connection. Think about a sports car that is teeming with power. Not slamming on the gas pedal and roaring from 0-60 can be painful. Just a small tap and you know that the car will leap forward. With all that engine power right there, you need to just sit there and wait while you prepare. You have to look at your map and plot the right course. If you don't, while you may still enjoy the feeling of driving fast—with the wheel in your hand and the air in your face—you are more likely to run out of fuel before you reach your destination.

As we subtly push the original marshmallow their way, allowing others to imbibe in instant gratification, we wait. We wait patiently for that second, and third, and fourth marshmallow.

When people learn that interacting with you is easy, enjoyable, and valuable, you become a welcome part of their life. Over time, you may even become an influencer in their lives. Because of this, your point of view, your reasoning, and your ability to inspire are all raised to new heights. By putting your desires on temporary hold, your point of view becomes infinitely more attractive!

"So why doesn't everyone put their desires on hold?"

At this point, I am afraid I have good news and bad news...

The good news: *Delaying gratification is not about talent... anyone can do it!*

The bad news: *It's not easy and takes a lot of practice.*

The ability to delay gratification is like a muscle: it can be developed. However, as anyone who has trained their muscles knows, the time and effort necessary to grow can be a painful process.

Once again, I have good news and bad news:

The good news: most people don't delay their gratifications, offering you the opportunity to gain a rare competitive advantage.

The bad news: there are going to be forces working against you or—more accurately—causing you to work against yourself. I call these forces "**gratification traps.**" These traps can be incredibly overwhelming depending on the nature of your character and your circumstances.

So what exactly is a gratification trap?

*A **gratification trap** is any conversational dynamic that tempts you to satisfy your need for instant gratification in a way that compromises your chances of persuading the other person or having a positive lasting impact on them.*

Over the years, I have identified several of these gratification traps:

1. A false sense of urgency;
2. A need for absolute certainty; and
3. A need for credit.

Every time you fall into one of these gratification traps, you've eaten a marshmallow so to speak. In doing so, you've kept it from the person you're interacting with.

Have you fallen into any of these gratification traps before? Let's find out.

How many times have you found yourself...?

- Raising your voice during a discussion?
- Cutting off the other person mid-sentence?
- Having a conversation that quickly devolves into a yelling match?
- Not letting the conversation end and insisting on saying "one last thing" when people indicate they want to end the conversation?

Sound familiar? It's no wonder that we frequently walk away from a really bad argument with a knot in our stomach or all worked up and upset. When you devour several pounds of marshmallows at once, you're bound to have a stomach ache!

| Chapter 4 |

A False Sense of Urgency

When we get drawn into a conversation that matters to us, it's easy to forget the about the rest of the world. Passion can absorb us and make it easy to forget that the person in front of us is actually a friend. And even if they are not a friend, but instead fall along the lines of a coworker, they are more than simply a person who disagrees with us on a specific issue. We forget that the outcome of this discussion will have little or no real impact on the world at large, but may have real impact on our lives in the context of our personal or work relationship with this person.

This isn't to say that being active and engaging with the people around you about things you care about isn't important or noble. Instead, I want to state that the outcome of each individual interaction is much less significant than it feels in the heat of the moment. The energy, effort, and pressures we often apply to these situations are nowhere near proportionate to the upside of actually getting them to agree.

If you saw someone's body language during a heated discussion, you might think that people's lives depended on the outcome of the conversation! This is the false sense of urgency which creeps in when we find ourselves invested in an idea or belief. This sense of urgency not only develops when we discuss issues with someone who believes the exact opposite, but sometimes it can be triggered by even the slightest opposition. It is the product of two emotions: fear, and a desire to impact the world around us and be meaningful.

Fear and eliminating (perceived) threats

When someone challenges our beliefs, an instinctive fear arises. That person automatically becomes a threat, regardless of how close they are to us. In fact, there is often a direct correlation between how close a person is to us and the intensity of the threat we feel when they disagree with us. For anybody who has read Shakespeare's *Julius Caesar*, the immortal words, "Et tu Brute" may come to mind.

When we feel threatened—or even just mildly uncomfortable—we automatically try to remove whatever threat there is to our safety. The sooner the better!

But, it is our ability to endure discomfort and maintain a steady hand as we navigate back to safe waters that will determine how quickly—and effectively—we get there. This ability is the very essence of delaying gratification.

Failure to remain calm and calculated will only reinforce the threat, allowing it to spiral into a consuming and vicious circle. The more threatened we feel, the more desperate we become to remove the threat. To do this, we increase pressure on the person we are trying to persuade. We raise our voice, our body language becomes more aggressive, and we cut them off mid-sentence and begin attacking *them*. The more pressure we apply, the more resistant they become. The more resistant they become... the more pressure we apply! In doing so, we become their threat and fuel the vicious cycle. Each of these behaviors only serves to reinforce the other person's contrary opinion, while also completely disrupting the Persuasion Equation.

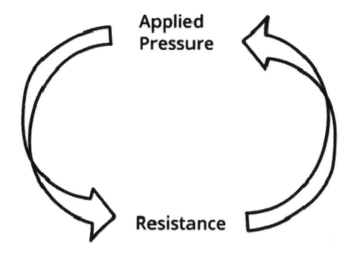

Applied Pressure

Resistance

The biggest tragedy in this vicious cycle is not only how counter-productive our attempts at persuasion are, but also that our conduct will have a devastating impact on future conversations with that person, discussions that will revolve around completely different issues.

An impending sense of urgency, one that tells us we have to convince them *right now*, can be the very thing that ensures someone else will never see things as we do.

Unrelenting pressure is incredibly unpleasant. When we are the ones applying it, we put ourselves in a situation where the other person is going to associate us with discomfort. They start to see us as "persuasion bullies," and might start avoiding us all altogether. There goes the Persuasion Equation.

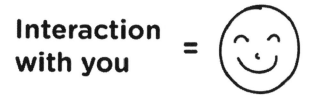

Interaction with you =

Our desire to impact the world and be meaningful

Wanting efficacy—*to know that our actions produce desired results*—leads us directly into a false sense of urgency. More than ever before, people seem to have a growing sense of not being able to affect the world around them. Feeling powerless can drive someone to push their point or act forcefully. Just think about how many times you raised your voice at a service provider who kept saying there was nothing they could do; you probably felt absolutely tiny as you lived out that horrible feeling of being a small speck of dust against a massive organization. Sure, they were extremely nice to you when they wanted your business. But now, when the phone is broken or the internet is down, it's you against this monster and there's nothing you can do about it. But there is. You can yell and make noise and insult the representative who keeps giving you the same broken record answer. Deep inside, you know all of the screaming and yelling in the world won't help. If anything, it will only serve to remove any hint of motivation the person you're speaking with may have to proactively help you find a solution.

One indication of this feeling of powerlessness is the steady global decline in voter turnout over the past several decades. It's becoming harder and harder to be heard in today's world, even in the face of the rise of social networks and new media platforms (maybe even due to these new global platforms). While these appear as communication tools and distribution channels that past generations could only dream of, they have a dark side. Though we feel as if our opinion is finally free to be shared to all the world, these outlets are promising the same to a staggering two billion people who are not just a potential audience, but also competing voices.

We used to live in a world where we met 50-150 people in our entire lives. Now we meet *thousands* and can reach *billions*.

When we engaged with those 50-150 people (everyone we would ever meet), none of them were listening to us while staring at the screens of their smart phones; we had their undivided attention. Ironically, as technological advances expanded our reach exponentially, it also shrank the attention we get from the very audiences it introduced us to.

We are "efficacy starved" and living in a world where attention is one of the scarcest resources. Discussions with people around us can be exactly what we are looking for—an outlet to address this feeling of powerlessness and insignificance.

When we are faced with the opportunity of persuading someone, we feel, "Finally, an opportunity to have a meaningful impact on the world!" When opportunity knocks, we grab it. Or, to be more accurate, *we bear hug it and squeeze it to death*. The opportunity to persuade someone over to our way of thinking, a chance to gain that ever-craved feeling of efficacy, is like water in the desert, like a drug to an addict, like food to a starving man. We have arrived at the source of this false sense of urgency and what makes this gratification trap so dangerous and disruptive.

The fact that this is one person out of billions does not prevent us from seeing them as the entire world, causing us to apply pressure accordingly.

Fight your intuition!

The way to avoid this gratification trap requires us to adopt a counter-intuitive approach. The stronger our sense of urgency, the more laid back we need to be. The more important the outcome of the conversation is to us, the more relaxed and patient we need to be.

Does this require practice? Yes! It can be hard as hell. But it is an acquired skill. Think of it as going to an emotion-gym. The more work you put in, the stronger you're going to be.

And, as your emotional intelligence grows, you will be capable of handling tougher situations. Conversations that had you pulling out your hair will become easier to endure as you approach them with a calm demeanor that works in your favor.

A great way to practice

Dedicate the next week to engaging with several people about topics you both care about. Seek out people with opinions that are contrary to yours. Then, start a conversation with them, but **do not** try and change their minds.

That's right!

Make the entire conversation about giving them the opportunity to convince you.

I repeat: do not try to change their minds during these conversations.

This may feel awkward, and may even be painful for you as the conversation evolves. Stay strong and hold the course! This is exactly what an "emotional workout" looks like.

Thanks to the reciprocal nature of human interaction, your conduct and attitude will, more times than not, be adopted by the other person and reflected back at you. Not only that, but by not posing a threat to them, you will actually be defusing their false sense of urgency.

Now, since both of you are more relaxed and feel safe, the entire exchange should become far more relaxed and might even be pleasant. This outcome, in and of itself, will have a *huge* impact on the outcome of the conversation—more so than any argument or fact you may present!

| Chapter 5 |

The Need for Absolute Certainty

It's been said that hindsight is 20/20. Looking back, I find it worthwhile to reflect not only on the things I learned as a competitive debater, but also on the important things I had to *unlearn*.

Perhaps the most important thing I had to unlearn was the idea that, in order to win, you have to defeat the team representing the opposing view. Not only defeat them, but crush them! I understand why winning and losing is required in a competitive setting, but applying that mentality to the real world is grounds for repeated failure.

Instead, the best forms of persuasion require that the person you are persuading be able to adopt your point of view without feeling defeated.

Furthermore, in real life, there is rarely a "winning" argument that decisively determines an absolute right and wrong, leaving all other arguments obsolete.

In fact, there are rarely issues that have a definitive right and wrong. Most issues tend to have *many* valid arguments that offer support to opinions from both sides of the aisle. The simple realization that not every conversation has to be a matter of black and white will open so many doors that you never imagined were there. Your ability to allow for the coexistence of opposing arguments, as well as the existence of imperfections within your worldview, will allow your relationships to deepen. More people will respect your consideration, and you will even open yourself to new ways of thinking—a critically important capacity in the rapidly-changing world of the 21st century. Interestingly, all of these approaches will enhance your ability to persuade others and bring them over to your way of seeing the world.

Another long-held belief I had to revise from my days of competitive debating was that persuasion is about solid argumentation and facts. Perhaps if we lived in a purely rational world, this might be true. **But we don't.** Instead, most of the decisions people make are non-rational. As we saw with emotional intelligence, the nature of your dynamic with the person you are trying to persuade carries *much more* weight than any logical argument or fact you might send their way.

And yet, I can't count how many times I have seen people arguing with one another with so much conviction as though there couldn't be any other way of thinking other than their own!

It is only fair that I confess that this has always been one of my worst weaknesses; overcoming my certainty that I was 100% right has been one of my greatest battles in life. The unrelenting certainty in the statements I made, frequently delivered with all the signs of battle (flushed faces, raised voices, and that piercing look in the eyes that shows a fury born of nightmares), is so complete that you would think the people involved were being guided by the hand of God!

Now, unlike the false sense of urgency trap—a pitfall that stems primarily from fear—this gratification trap, needing the comfort of absolute certainty, comes from overwhelming amounts of passion and exaggerated self-confidence.

In our defense, I could argue that this predisposition is cultivated in us from when we are little kids. As we watch cartoons and Disney movies, portraying heroes and villains in such a clear dichotomy, a belief in a black and white world is cultivated. The same can be said about old westerns, in which the symbolic white and black hats indicate who the good guys are and who we should be cheering against. Then, as we grow up and go to school, we are evaluated through standardized testing methods that expect one right answer for each question. This indoctrination persists through our aging into adulthood and by then is deeply rooted in us.

And maybe it's not all bad, after all, life seems so much easier when there are clear boundaries between right or wrong. When things aren't certain, and there are many choices, decision making can be an absolute nightmare!

Just think about the process of choosing a shampoo or laundry detergent or breakfast cereal when you have five dozen brands competing for your attention!

When it comes to politics, the range of options—and the stakes associated with these options—becomes infinitely more complicated. It would seem that the first two decades of the 21st century have the sole intention of presenting western leaders with impossible dilemmas, with each course of action somehow violating a sacred moral principle or pillar.

For instance, with conflicts in the Middle East, and the heartbreaking ethnic wars they have led to in countries like Syria and Iraq, who should the west support: the rebels fighting against oppressive dictatorships, or the dictatorships being rebelled against by religious fundamentalists who stand against the very foundations of the western world? Each option has its share of upsides to meet its litany of gaping holes. Even the ancient proverb, "The enemy of my enemy," no longer offers clarity in today's mad and highly-complex reality.

And yet, in spite of each path having highly complex—and frequently unforeseen—consequences, most of the views heard on major US media outlets are presented with an absolute tone. Turn on the news after any major strife and you will undoubtedly hear statements such as, "Obama *had to* bring down Syrian dictator Assad after his use of chemical weapons against the rebels!" and "Thank God Obama didn't send advanced weapons to the Syrian rebels, otherwise they would have been aimed back at us shortly after!"

Here are two directly opposing points of view with a worrying similarity—absolute certainty. Our horrible discomfort with uncertainty leads us to find refuge in bold statements and declared certainty, *even when it is not really there*. Thus, the more uncertain the path, the more assertive the opinions that are expressed.

These absolute statements are a gratification trap. More often than not, they do not assist us in persuading others, nor do they lead us to the best course of action. Instead, they often reinforce a counterproductive outcome in which we are seen as arrogant, shallow, or fear-mongering.

It's time for our emotional intelligence to kick in once again! Our innate desire is going to cause us to lean on behaviors that strive to eliminate our discomfort as quickly as possible. In light of our fears of being wrong, the most convenient and readily available solution is to apply *complete certainty* to our point of view and defend it with everything we've got.

Adopting a stance that says, "*I am completely certain that I am right!*" may grant you instant emotional relief—which is why it's a gratification trap—but it also has the power to taint your relationship with the person you are trying to persuade in the following ways:

You come across as cocky and condescending

We have all been around people who think they know *everything*, as well as people who are so damn sure of themselves that you just want to smack them! As intelligent and educated as they may be, they're probably also the last person on earth you would concede a point to. Winston Churchill captured this perfectly when he said, "*Personally I'm always ready to learn, although I do not always like being taught.*"

Nobody likes to be outsmarted, and as people, we will go to great lengths to avoid feeling inadequate. If you make people feel stupid, or create a situation where they can't effectively share their thoughts, you will quickly become an antagonist in their story. People aren't usually too fond of interacting with someone that makes them feel small. Antagonists are often seen as negative people who leave negative memories with the people they are affecting. This is not effective in the least for persuading someone else to come over to your way of thinking.

Put frankly, being a know-it-all makes it *very hard* to sit back and listen to all of the "wrong things" the other person is saying as they delay the enlightenment you are itching to share.

If people don't want to be around or engage with you, any hopes of bringing them over to your side are brought to a screeching halt and future conversations are tossed behind locked doors.

It seems like you are hogging the conversation

A firm belief that you already have the right answer to anything that challenges your opinions eliminates any need for you to actually listen to them. This can be a huge hiccup for meaningful persuasion. Coming back to the idea of reciprocity, if you don't bother to listen to them, why should they listen to you? Listening to a person giving an ongoing monologue erases any opportunity you might feel there is for real discourse. It seems more like you are standing on a soapbox yelling at the peons below.

After all, every second they are speaking is really just a waste of time. I mean… they are going to hear what you have to say, and it will undoubtedly hit them like a bolt of lightning just how right you are! So why let them speak at all? It seems like a shame to allow for any delays in their path to enlightenment… right?

Wrong! So, so wrong.

The person you are conversing with may be just as sure of their own opinion as you are of yours. Once you start competing with them for the "microphone," they will not be emotionally able to reach a middle ground with you, mainly because they will feel deprived of their opportunity to make a difference. Any points you made that they might have otherwise adopted—or even just considered—are lost, because now they feel that very same all-consuming need to win.

The moral of the story? Share the damn microphone!

Don't miss "Yes" opportunities

People need to live with the outcome of a persuasive interaction well after the interaction has ended. Most of us don't necessarily consider the emotional, social, and practical aftermath for the person we have persuaded. This aftermath can be especially difficult when regarding heavily-charged moral or political topics.

Opinions are more than mere intellectual stances. What we hold true reflects a way of life and are part of our place in a greater social echo system. It is a meaningful part of who we are, of our very identity. Beyond the fact that being persuaded requires us to accept that we were wrong about something and that that we have spent a portion of our life "living the wrong way." Then, we must also go back to our own world and confront the people we have an expansive history with. Some of these relationships are likely to be built on foundational beliefs that we have shared for as long as we can remember. And now, these foundations have been shaken, maybe even shattered. *That is the price of persuasion,* and it is a big unseen force that can work against our persuasive efforts.

Note: These persuasive dynamics aren't the kind that are going to be found in common workplace discussions or simple day-to-day interactions. Instead, these are the kind of interactions that we find on our campuses and around our dinner tables. They are the kind of discussions that pertain to *grand social, financial, political, and moral issues.*

Coming to terms with the reality that you have been "wrong" for so long is not an emotionally easy thing to do. In fact, in certain cases, the emotional cost of accepting a competing point of view is so intense that we develop defense mechanisms to shut down any internal willingness to listen to, let alone accept, that point of view. We might even reinforce our stand to the extent that we completely disregard even the most obvious and compelling evidence in support of that competing view. This is known as "cognitive dissonance," and the more confident you allow yourself to be, the more susceptible you are to not hearing a word the other person says, no matter how reasonable or well-founded it might be!

What this boils down to is that being right and bathing in the comfort of certainty—as gratifying as they may be in the heat of the moment—*will not improve our chances at lasting persuasion.* Instead, they are far more likely to impede our ability to persuade people around us and trigger cognitive dissonance. At the end of the day, the fact that we have a clear opinion and a burning passion is what drives us into persuasive conversations. And yet, when left unchecked, that same passion and devotion can be the very things that stand in the way of actually persuading the people we interact with.

So how do I stop it?

To avoid letting the blaze roar out of control, our emotional intelligence needs to kick in and apply a healthy dose of self-control. Then, we can use our passion to give us the patience to trade opportunities—instant gratification for them in return for true lasting impact for us.

As soon as we enter into a conversation where we want to persuade the other person, we need to make a conscious decision to temporarily adopt doubt about our own "rightness." At first, this might feel insincere, but in time—and with the incredible results that this kind of approach rewards—it will ultimately become an entirely sincere approach. It will become a habit that will do much more than help us persuade people; it will make us better decision makers all together (cognitive dissonance is a notorious flaw in decision-making processes. People who develop the ability to minimize its impact emerge as powerful decision makers).

The first step is the exact same as the one I recommended as a defense against the false sense of urgency gratification trap: put *your* opinions and *your* needs on hold. Let the other person go first. Provide the person you are trying to persuade with frequent instant gratification, and let it pave a path to the desired lasting impact on them.

This will:

- Reduce the chances of you tumbling headfirst into this gratification trap;
- Enhance the other person's overall willingness to listen to you afterward (this is reciprocity in play); and
- Create a positive impression of you in their mind. Instead of you coming across as stubborn, arrogant, and condescending, you will more likely be experienced and later remembered as someone who is moderate, open-minded, and generally pleasant and easy to talk to. The benefits of this long-term strategy are in the development of your personal brand. Furthermore, on the occasion that you do express yourself with greater assertiveness, you will be taken more seriously and the words you say will be held in higher regard. This does not guarantee their automated consent, but will undoubtedly increase the consideration your words will receive. That, my friends, is an amazing reward for the foregoing of short-lived instant gratification.

| Chapter 6 |

The Need for Credit

Here's the situation: your team has been debating the best way to secure a deal with a client. The question on the table: should a discount be offered in an effort to encourage the client to close the deal faster?

This discussion has been going on for two weeks and you are getting *really tired* of the same arguments being presented over and over again. The team seems to be going in circles. From the start, you've said that time to market (TTM) is key from a strategic point of view, and that the sooner the deal gets closed, the better, even if it requires a dramatic discount.

Other people on your team think differently. They are concerned about the long-term impact of a price reduction and how it might reflect on the company. Coming in with a discount might set an expectation for this client to always insist on a price reduction, not to mention the negative effect on the positioning of the solution your company is bringing to the market; "You want your price point to match the clients you are targeting," one person says. Another pipes up, "Pricing is important for branding and positioning, and a discount at this point in time will be harmful."

So far so good from a persuasion point of view. Up to this point, you have practiced patience and pushed yourself to not fall into the false sense of urgency and need for absolute certainty gratification traps.

First, you waited until others expressed their opinions. This allowed you to get a better idea of the team's variety of opinions, and let you take note of where individual members stood. Even after several arguments directly clashing with your opinion were put out there, you kept a healthy distance from the traps. You asked follow-up questions that gave team members (especially the ones who held a contrary opinion to yours) the opportunity to further explain the validity of their points of view. To this, you get a resounding "Great job!" from me.

Next, you continued to delay your own gratification by acknowledging the opinions that were presented, and even chose to reinforce them with examples of how lowering prices as a market-penetration strategy can have negative mid-to-long-term consequences. Only then—once you successfully laid out your expertise of all available options—did you go on to explain that the risk in this specific case is much lower than other cases would indicate. You are now 2/2! This is the ultimate way of avoiding the need for absolute certainty gratification trap. You rock!

Still, no consensus was reached. The meeting ended and another was scheduled. Several days later, you find yourself sitting in yet another team meeting about this particular pricing dilemma. Time is running out and decisions need to be made.

Suddenly, one of your colleagues says, "You know, all things considered, I think we should give them this discount. I think that if we close this deal before the end of the quarter, it will allow us to meet our projected profit targets and get us some favorable reviews from the analysts. It will also free up our attention to focus on the other two clients we want to close and maybe even get them to sign within the next three months. I really don't think the general concerns of giving such a discount need to worry us for this specific case."

You listen, thinking to yourself, *"You're wasting your breath my friend."* Instead, following a short silence, the rest of the team nods in agreement. *"I agree,"* comes from one end of the table. Another voice is added to the mix, *"I think we are overthinking this. It's just one deal and we should move fast."* Another compliments your colleague, *"So glad you could attend today, we were going in circles around this."* Everybody nods again. It has been agreed, and the client will be given the discount.

Something inside you snaps. That's the final straw!

Blood boiling in your veins and a ringing in your ears, you lunge into a gratification trap head first: *"**HE** is right? Really!? Are you **kidding** me!? I've been saying that for the last two weeks!"*

Everyone turns to you in surprise. Silence.

Your frustrations rushing to the surface, that knee-jerk outburst has just undermined all of the hard work you have put in up to this point. Allow me to introduce the third gratification trap: our need for credit.

What's uniquely tragic about this gratification trap is that, while the other two distance us from those who disagree with us, this one puts us at odds with those who actually agree with us. While the other two delay the reaching of a consensus, this one actually delays the implementation of an already-reached and desirable consensus.

Instead of being happy that the right decision was made, and that your point of view was ultimately endorsed—likely bringing about positive results for the company—you erupted, turning a positive outcome into a negative experience for everyone involved. And the one person that championed the belief you were promoting, has been alienated in the process. You've turned your ally into a foe.

This is, clearly and unfortunately, a major blow to your future interactions with your team members. Just like that; persuading them of anything in the future has turned into an uphill battle.

Where did it all go wrong?

In reality, it's not too difficult to argue that this wasn't really your fault. Think about it… what are we taught from the very first day of first grade and until the last day of our graduate studies? How are we measured by the educational institutions where we spent so many of our formative years? How do employers justify our worth? The answer to each of these questions is the source of the third, and most difficult-to-overcome, gratification trap, our need for credit!

In school, we are taught that the right answers result in good grades (the kind mom and dad are likely to pin on the fridge). The better our grades, the better the universities we get into, and that will help determine the jobs we get. At work, we need credit for our professional contributions to justify raises and promotions (not to mention a legendary reputation amongst our colleagues and peers). In all of these situations, a dynamic of scarcity is involved. After all, only one can be Valedictorian. There are only a limited number of scholarships and even just regular admission slots to go around. There is only one "Employee of the Month" and there are fewer and fewer possible positions as you climb the corporate ladder to that ever narrowing top of the organizational pyramid.

In short, throughout our lives, we are taught that there is a direct correlation between being acknowledged and getting credit and being successful (and being happy, of course. Which, in fact (and very sadly), has little to do with professional success in many cases. But we don't know that until we get there and it drives us deep into this tragic gratification trap).

While credit might be necessary for educational institutions to set a standard, or for workplaces to determine the value of their workers, linking credit with success could not be more wrong when it comes to persuasion. In fact, a storehouse of credit for being a highly persuasive individual is more likely to hamper our ability to persuade. For anyone aware of our persuasion "track record," it can even be an anchor that pulls us down, as they approach conversations with us with greater apprehension. This expectation people come to have of us is called our "messenger status," and it greatly influences the starting point of our interactions with them. It also affects the overall chances we have of successfully persuading them. As a "professional persuader," I am, ironically, doomed to have to make an ever-greater effort to persuade people, because they "see me coming" a mile away. From my point of view, there is nothing to "see," as I believe that true persuasion is a mutual search for win-win solutions. But most people misunderstand the process of persuasion and perceive is as a competitive dynamic. As such, they "brace for impact" and raise their guard when any form of dialogue is initiated with me, as soon as there is a hint of persuasion in the air.

Make it happen, captain

Society and upbringing be damned! Once again, and as is the case for all gratification traps, we must combine self-control with a conscious effort to unlearn and let go of bad habits. Even though we have been thoroughly indoctrinated to see urgency, certainty, and credit as valuable, they are holding us back when it comes to effective persuasion. It's time to wrestle back control.

When we wish to persuade, our ability to have lasting influence over the people in our lives is almost completely dependent on us *not* getting the credit. Unlike competitive settings (which any conversations involving opposing views will innately feel like), our ability to persuade is almost entirely dependent on our willingness to establish a conversation as a collaboration instead of a competition—a search for truth, not for victory. And, when our opinions are accepted by the other person, it is our role to ensure that they do not feel defeated or beaten, but rather content and enlightened. If we can infuse them with a sense of ownership for the conclusions of the conversation, then we have truly succeeded. At the cost of credit, we have secured true lasting impact. Ownership over a conclusion breeds a greater willingness to defend it against future challengers.

At all costs, we need to avoid soaking in too much credit. And, whatever you do, **stay away from "I told you so" statements!** Self-congratulation is the quickest detonator for any progress that has been made.

It is the complete clash between the role of credit in our daily lives (as ingrained in us by society) and its place in persuasive dynamics that makes this gratification trap so very dangerous. Avoiding this gratification trap boils down to the same fundamental choice we have been looking at since the start of this book: a choice between instant gratification (in this case—getting credit, being acknowledged, feeling powerful, and worthy) and lasting influence. It's about choosing who will bask in the spotlight during these interactions—you... or them.

Striking out in the opposite direction

The highest level of persuasion is *when the other person ends up thinking that they came up with the conclusion themselves or that agreeing with you is simply a further reinforcement of values or principles they had already held.*

Imagine participating in a group discussion and not presenting *even one statement*. Consider what it would be like to assume the role of facilitator, presiding over the conversation and only presenting open-ended questions from time-to-time. Each of these questions, carefully thought out and perfectly executed, would gradually lead members of the group down a cognitive and emotional path until they ultimately find themselves at the conclusion you have lead them to. Only, from their perspective, they found the way to these conclusions on their own.

That is true influence.

From my experience as a professional facilitator, I can tell you that this form of persuasion can be extremely frustrating to carry out. It requires a kind of patient and result-oriented approach that is faintly reminiscent of secret agents and superhe-

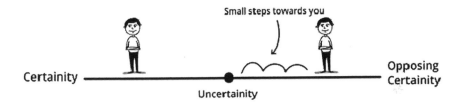

roes. They constantly save the day, and yet they never receive the celebration they deserve. It is only a positive outcome that they can derive satisfaction from.

For those of us with a large ego to feed and who are significantly more knowledgeable about the topics being discussed—like yours truly—this can be insanely frustrating. Not only do these attributes drive a strong need for credit (gratification trap #3), but they also rope in a strong sense of absolute certainty (gratification trap #2).

Combining two traps means double the trouble. Here you are, discussing something you have read volumes about, a topic you have discussed with dozens, if not hundreds, of people before, and yet you can't shout what you're thinking— "Listen to me! I'm an expert" —if you wish to have lasting impact.

It gets worse! Given the number of times that you have had this conversation, you even know—almost to a T—exactly how the conversation will progress: which points will be introduced first, which objections will then be given, and so on.

And yet, to avoid this devious gratification trap:

- You are **NOT** going to be the first to speak or present a decisive opinion.
- You are **NOT** going to hog the conversation.
- You are **NOT** going to be the first to respond to or defuse any statement contrary to your opinion.

When you speak, try to (at least at first) only use open-ended questions. For the event we have been looking at, consider how the following questions would open the table for discussion:

Q: What are our options right now?

Q: What's more important to us at this point in time:

a) Cash flow?

b) Our current quarterly sales targets?

c) Our pricing positioning beyond this specific deal?

d) Creating the right foundations for the ongoing relationship with this specific client?

If we agree on our end goal, it may be easier for us to decide…

Q: Is there a way for us to give the client the discount without it being perceived as a discount?

Q: What negative outcomes should we be concerned with if we don't give the client this discount?

Q: What negative outcomes should we be concerned with if we give the client this discount?

When used properly, open-ended questions (which let us play the neutral ground) allow for a much more productive conversation. And, when used wisely, these questions will also steer the conversation ever-so-gradually toward the conclusion you believe in. And all of this will be done without this outcome being directly attributed to you. In fact, you will know that you played your part perfectly if, at the end of the discussion, people are not entirely sure what your original stance was.

When it comes to the need for credit gratification trap, overcoming it requires a great deal more from your facilitation skills than the false sense of urgency or sense of absolute certainty gratification traps.

Above and beyond the emotional endurance required to avoid this gratification trap, there is yet another challenge—leading a dialogue or group discussion without actually being asked to act as facilitator is tricky. We need to manage a way of doing so while steering clear of appearing condescending. Another challenge is using the right questions in a way that keeps them truly open ended, but also leads the conversation in the right direction by focusing on the right considerations.

When used in the service of persuasion, good facilitation is about:

- Knowing when to intervene with a question;

- Knowing which question to ask;

- Knowing who should be the recipient of your question;

- Knowing the answers to these listed questions in the context of group dynamics; and

- Having killer analytical skills to design a path of questions that will likely lead to your desired outcome.

You might be thinking, "Ariel, that sounds incredibly intense. I don't think I have that kind of tact or skill set. Does this doom me as an effective persuader?"

No way! Even if you don't have the time, natural predisposition, or simply the inclination to become a professional facilitator, you can still practice and find incredible levels of success. Remember, your EQ-related ability to **control your own conduct** is a comprehensive ability that will help you avoid all three gratification traps. And, just like any other muscle, growth is dramatic and opens up a new world of possibilities.

Holstering the Gun

Sarah looked down at her messenger bag, the corner of one of her event brochures poking its head out. *"Hopefully I won't need that,"* she thought to herself. Looking around the room at the rich leather couches and mahogany-stained bookshelves, she couldn't help but think that it was nice to be a freelance event planner; not everybody else was able to see so many different offices.

"Miss Peters, Jenny will see you now."

Sarah Peters smiled at the receptionist and made her way into Jenny's office. A small door plaque read "Jennifer Dawkins—SVP of Human Resources." Opening the door, she was greeted by a smiling woman in her mid-40's. Taking a seat opposite to Jenny, Sarah started things off. *"Thanks for meeting with me! I can imagine how busy you must be."*

Jenny waved the comment away, *"Don't mention it. Any friend of Jack is a friend of mine! Why don't you tell me a little more about what you do?"*

Lightly kicking her messenger bag under her seat, stuffed with different brochures and pamphlets, Sarah took a breath, *"How about I give you a 60-second overview and then you can tell me what you would like me to expand on based on your needs?"*

Jenny nodded, *"Sure, go ahead."*

Here it was, the moment of truth. *"From my experience over the past 20 years, one of the biggest mistakes I see is people believing that budget is the biggest challenge for putting on an event. It isn't. From my experience, when producing events, the main concern is the security of knowing that all aspects pertaining to quality, timeliness, and attendance are fully met and aligned with the purpose of the event--making sure that a real ROI (Return On Investment) is brought about; this is all within the given budget, of course! That's where I come in. Every production I manage begins with defining the ROI in as many details as possible. Then, and only then, I reverse engineer from the ROI to every last detail of the event itself."*

Based on the slight wince on Jenny's face, the points had clearly hit the mark. *"Well, budget definitely is a pain. But I have to say that I agree. Unfortunately, the last event we produced, while staying within budget, completely missed the mark. We got low satisfaction reviews from the employees and the CEO. We definitely have to do better on our next event."*

Sarah took a breath and made sure not to jump the gun. *"If you don't mind me asking, what exactly were you unhappy with?"*

An hour later, after having discussed the many failings of the previous event and how they can be prevented in the future, Jenny closed the meeting: *"Thanks so much for your valuable input, Sarah, you clearly know your stuff. And, more importantly, it is obvious that you love what you do."*

"I do," said Sarah. *"I am very lucky to have found what I love!"*

The following morning, Sarah was delighted to find an email from Jenny in her inbox introducing her to one of the HR managers on Jenny's team. It read, "Hey Mike, following our brief conversation in our weekly yesterday, please connect with Sarah to see how she can help us with our November event." That was it. A short email that signaled the beginning of a long and prosperous relationship.

TAKEAWAY: It's never about you. Even when you are invited to present your product, service, or opinion, it is still about the person in front of you. Don't hog the microphone! Spend more time listening than speaking, especially in the early stages of a relationship. Sarah's success hinged on putting Jenny's needs in the spotlight, not her own. Focusing on **who Jenny is** and **what she needs** rather than placing the majority of the conversation on who Sarah is and what she is selling was the key to success. This is what turned a 20-minute courtesy meeting into a one-hour long "value discovery" conversation that allowed Sarah a better insight to Jenny's needs. It also allowed Jenny to experience, rather than just hear about, Sarah's expertise and professional abilities. Whenever you are trying to sell a product or service, focus on the value it brings the buyer rather than on the attributes of the object itself (and yes, focusing on what is important to you is missing the mark by a mile! Remember, this is all about them).

| Chapter 7 |

A Safety Net

N ow that we understand the importance of delayed gratification and are better equipped to identify looming gratification traps, let's take a step forward and learn how to systematically avoid them!

In the following chapter, I will share five key practices that you can use to actively avoid gratification traps and develop your powers of persuasion. By allowing yourself to adopt a mindset of patience, you create an opportunity to navigate the intricate and winding paths of persuasion, eventually arriving at some exceptionally green pastures!

Key Practice #1: Persuasion is a process

Take your time. Understanding that *real persuasion is a process that can take hours—sometimes even months—*is one of the best ways to avoid the false sense of urgency gratification trap. Just take a deep breath and give yourself some room to navigate. Frantically pushing your opinion on others gives you very little room to operate.

How many times have we gotten lost in a debate and felt (and even behaved) as if it was the most important conversation in the world? As tunnel vision kicks in, we somehow come to believe that nothing is more important than getting the person in front of us to accept our point of view *right now*!

We've all been there.

But, when you stop to think about it for a second, you may start to understand that the majority of discussions have no need to turn into a shouting match. Frankly, it doesn't do any good for anyone involved! And even if it does feel good, in the moment, to shout and tackle the other person head on, nobody likes to be shouted at. Think about it, no matter the outcome of the debate, it's not likely to change the outcome of the world (unless the person you are debating is the President of the United States!).

If the last paragraph seemed obvious and almost condescending, just think about the last heated debate you had, whether it was with a friend, a loved one, or a work colleague. It's not about understanding what I wrote is right; after all, this is not an IQ-related challenge. Instead, it is an EQ challenge, one that requires we be able to act precisely in the heat of the moment.

Now ask yourself, if the person you were debating was suddenly struck by spontaneous wisdom—realizing how absolutely right you have been throughout the entire debate—what consequence would that have on either of your lives? Would it change the world around you?

Consider the opposite. What if that person maintained their point of view with unwavering vigilance and wouldn't budge an inch? What consequences would that have on either of your lives? How would it change the world around you?

Don't get me wrong, I am not saying that the entire conversation between you and the other person is meaningless, or that you should not care what the outcome is. After all, *this book is about how to effectively, and efficiently, persuade people.* Instead, this principle is about managing expectations in order to not become your own obstacle on the way to meaningful persuasion and influence.

When we lose sight of the marginal, yet important, changes that come from each and every encounter, it's easy to find ourselves left wanting at the end of a conversation, and we might be tempted to break out into a full-on sprint. Sadly, as we apply more and more pressure to the other person, we influence them to take bigger steps... in the opposite direction we are aiming for!

And, of course, if the other person still doesn't concede, we apply even more pressure! However, as we all know, the more pressure you put on something, the more likely it is to become irrevocably damaged, sometimes even exploding and hurting us in the process.

This is the vicious cycle that can be avoided by approaching persuasion as a process.

By slowing down, you ensure that you won't lose control of yourself and of the conversation. If you consider that you will have additional opportunities to speak with this person, you are likely to naturally be more relaxed in your conversation with them. If you are not sure that you will have another opportunity to speak with this person, then your initial objective is to inspire a desire to stay in touch and speak again in the near future. Doing so should be easier than "converting" them within the span of a single conversation and creates a larger window of opportunity to achieve the desired conversion. Adopting this approach will ensure that you are far less likely to fall into the false sense of urgency gratification trap.

If lasting influence is our goal, we should aim to run a marathon, allowing the cumulative effect of really positive experiences with us to lead to incredible rewards down the road. After all, as is known in the world of startups, the greater the potential return on investment, the longer the justifiable "runway."

Losing the Sale of a Lifetime

"Oh my God... how can people be so blind?" Jessica was just about ready to storm out of the room. She glared at John from across the table as he ran his hands through his hair in a single stressed-out motion.

It was late, much later than she had planned on leaving the office, and there was no way that tired minds were helping. The later it got, the less patience she had, and John was not making things easier. Checking her watch, she sighed. 9:00 P.M. This meeting was supposed to be finished two hours ago!

"Jessica, it's basic accounting: there is no way we can go lower on this. We would be running at a loss... not to mention how this deal would look to our other clients. Next thing we know, everyone is clamoring for a discount and our margins are shot." John shook his head slightly the whole time he was speaking.

Jessica's face was an array of frustrated and disapproving expressions throughout John's monologue. Groaning audibly, she met his eyes. *"This is not just 'another client,* John! My team and I have been working on this deal for 16 months. 16 grueling months. We need this client. Take the longer view for once in your life. This deal is a drop in the bucket compared to the potential business we can get from them in the next 3-5 years. Stop being such a bean counter for five minutes and start thinking strategically. I swear... you finance people..."*

John's eyes narrowed. His face was red, but he took a deep breath and explained in a low, measured voice. *"Sales don't matter. Profit matters. Cash flow matters. This is a bad deal. 16 months, huh? Where were you all this time? I don't remember being invited to the planning meetings for this account. Did you not once think that maybe one of my people should have been there with you when you formulated the financials of this deal? Did you not think finance had something to say about the deal structure you sent them a good 14 months ago? No... this is sales after all. You got it all covered. Who cares about insignificant details like "profit" or "price-related market positioning" as long as you reach your sales goals, right!?"*

They both sat quietly for a few moments. Jessica wanted to kick herself. She had promised that she would not get into another one of these arguments with John. He was a good guy, she knew that. He was also a great finance manager. A superstar actually. But she had to get this deal approved and she knew that if she had gone to him earlier, it might have killed the process with the client early onboard.

"Let's just go over the numbers one more time so we can get the hell out of here." She had intended to say that in a tone that would ease the tension in the room, but it didn't come out that way.

Another hour spent huddled over spreadsheets and forecasts did little to find common ground; Instead, they both walked away wildly frustrated. The following morning, Jessica received a calendar notification from John indicating he needed to reschedule their Wednesday meeting. "Something came up," was all it said; no alternative time was suggested. Jessica knew this would cost her another four weeks at the very least. She would get the deal approved, even if it meant taking it directly to the CEO, who never let a deal go. But it would cost her: not only would it not be in time for this quarter's numbers, but it would come back to bite her in future dealings with John. Plus, the need to escalate this to the CEO would reflect badly on her in upcoming executive reviews. This was far from the outcome she wanted.

TAKEAWAY: Before I provide the takeaway for this story, let me begin by acknowledging how hard it is to work in large enterprises nowadays. Many of these massive, international and multicultural organizations are not structured to breed internal harmony. Different domain-centric units (HR, IT, Finance, Procurement, Quality Assurance, etc.) are tasked with siloed goals that sometimes even conflict directly with the goals of other units within the company. Amazingly, the very same executive leadership that gave them these conflicting goals then hires companies like mine to improve internal collaboration and coordinated execution. It's not a small problem, and it costs companies' tremendous amounts of money in lost productivity.

Nevertheless, in this case, Jessica brought this problem on herself. She did it by keeping John's team out of the loop earlier in the sales process. Maybe she was hoping that she could bend his will rather than truly mobilize it, given that he would be in the uncomfortable position of blocking a sealed deal. Perhaps it was because she wanted control over the process... who knows. It's even possible that it was all about getting the credit. Whatever her reasons, Jessica knowingly disregarded the interests of John's team in favor of hers. It just so happens that units or departments within organizations can have interests just the same as individuals do. The basic principles of persuasion still apply. Had Jessica understood, from day one of this deal materializing, that she needed to persuade John as much as she did her client, the outcome might be very different. Had she adopted persuasion as a process, getting John involved early on and even allowing him to build a sense of ownership over this deal, one of three things would have happened: 1) John would have raised his concerns much earlier and the terms of the deal may have been improved 2) John would have raised his concerns much earlier and Jessica could have backed away before accumulating a level of investment (real and psychological) that made it infinitely more difficult for her to walk away 3) John would have gained a deeper, more nuanced understanding of the company's strategic value for the deal, and possibly even developed a personal desire to see it through. Not only did Jessica back herself into a corner on the deal, but she also undermined the foundation of her ability to win John over in future cases.

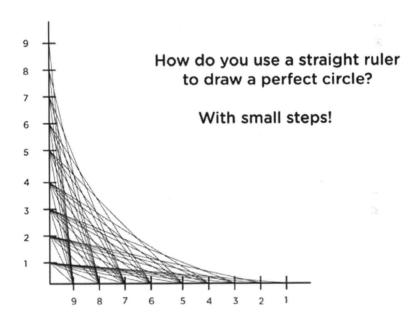

How do you use a straight ruler to draw a perfect circle?

With small steps!

Key Practice #2: Small steps

This quarter circle is not made of 1 line but rather 45. Each of these 45 lines represents a small step with which a perfectly straight line can create a perfect circle. That's exactly what this principle of "Small Steps" represents. Some people may seem rigid in their thinking. If you want to bend their thinking - use small steps.

Once you understand and accept the importance of adopting a process-oriented approach to persuasion, you can afford to create a more effective and thought-out strategy. Instead of asking yourself, "What's the most I can do to change this person's beliefs in *this* conversation?" you can ask, "What are the various "stations" I can take this person through on the path to where I want them to be?"

The name of this second principle pretty much speaks for itself. In many cases, the fact that opinions or outlook on life can be parts of our identity—how we perceive ourselves and where it places us in our social circles—can make it so that change is exceptionally hard to adopt. With beliefs being such a strong part of who we are, any new way of thinking can be jarring and cause us to hug tightly to the foundation we already have in place. It is this predisposition that fuels the need for absolute certainty gratification trap.

Changing someone's opinion on a purely intellectual level, especially about an issue that has no real impact on their lives, is very easy compared to getting someone to agree to change their behavior and identity. This is why it is critically important that, before we get all fired up and launch into our point of view (which of course holds all of the brilliant arguments to demonstrate just how right we are), we take an imaginary step back, and try to get a solid understanding of how far the other person's opinions are from the ones we are representing.

Take a second and imagine that every issue has two polar extremes, with a line connecting one to the other.

Now let's take a look at the questions that should determine your approach to the entire conversation:

1. Do you know how far their position is from the middle point?

2. Can you impartially estimate how far **you** are from the middle point?

Knowing where your position lies relative to the middle point—as well as how far the person you are communicating with is from this point—is crucial for effective engagement. And, if you are conducting this debate in front of an audience, this becomes even more crucial. This is because most mainstream and undecided audiences are most likely to want to associate themselves with the most moderate speaker.

Trying to appeal to a person that is hostile to your way of thinking can be disastrous if you don't take the time to discover this predisposition and adapt your strategy accordingly. As every good poker player knows, you play the opponent, not the hand.

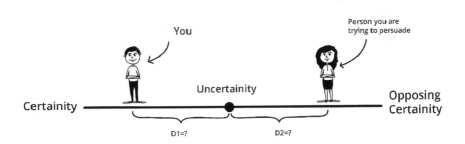

Once you have properly estimated how strongly the person (or people) you are communicating with hold to their opinion, you can effectively determine the size of the steps you plan on breaking the process into in order to draw them towards you.

Did you notice that I wrote toward you?

When most people argue, they do so in a way that expects the other person to rocket over the uncertainty point and arrive almost instantly at their position.

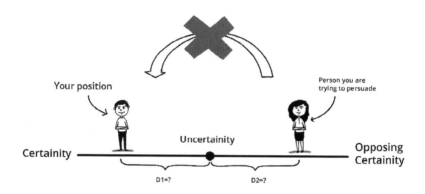

This doesn't work!

For a person to adopt a position contrary to their own, they must first have a reason to be uncertain of their own opinion. In other words, they must pass through the center point of "uncertainty," taking little baby steps until they eventually arrive at your position. Some of these steps, especially in longer and more strategic persuasion processes, may not even deal directly with the subject matter at hand and will be limited to **preliminary bonding** and **trust building** interactions (such as small talk, which is anything but "small" in its potential contribution to our chances of persuading and even long-term relationship building).

It is in the process of managing our expectations with ourselves (prior and during the early stage of the conversation) and understanding that we aren't going to just grab someone and have them immediately adopt our way of thinking, that allows us to properly establish the Persuasion Equation.

Once we understand that we are only trying to get them to take a small step at a time, and cover only a portion of the distance between us in a single "session", we can more easily calm the fighting "beast" within us, the inner voice that drives us to persuasion in the first place. We can then more easily create an enjoyable and pressure-free conversation.

But still a question looms: how do we know how to properly set our expectations? How do we determine how big or small the next step we expect of them should be?

The answer is fairly simple. The further from the center point of uncertainty either of you are, the smaller the first step you should have them take towards you. The first steps are crucially important in that they frame the person's general experience and expectation for the remainder of the process.

When people are not pushed or bullied into adopting a point of view, but are instead given the opportunity to walk through the process *and reach the conclusions themselves*, they are much more likely to develop a real sense of ownership over their new point of view. This makes the change both stronger in the immediate future and longer-lasting.

This principle of taking small steps directly negates all three gratification traps, protecting you from making others feel that you are yanking them out of their comfort zone and possibly making them feel stupid or rigid. Thus, you avoid being tagged as an undesired antagonist.

From a purely practical standpoint, if others don't want to be around us or don't wish to engage with us, what chance do we have of bringing them over to our way of thinking?

On the other hand, if you seem to be enjoying the conversation and are open to listening to the other person's point of view, they are left with a really positive memory of you. They will remember this memory of you for a much longer time than what you said or even what they thought about it.

By this point in the book, we have focused on encouraging and enabling people to change their minds. But what if there was a way to persuade others that didn't even require them to alter their way of thinking?

Key Practice #3: People are best persuaded by conclusions they have already reached themselves.

Admittedly, this is perhaps the most complex principle to master. How do you engage with a person, someone who appears to support a point of view in opposition to yours, and get them to agree with you without ever thinking that they have actually changed their mind?

The most effective form of persuasion is when you can get someone to agree with you without feeling defeated. Not only that, but to bring them over to your side without them even feeling persuaded. Your ultimate success will come if they adopt your point of view as being fully consistent with their *existing* values and *belief system*.

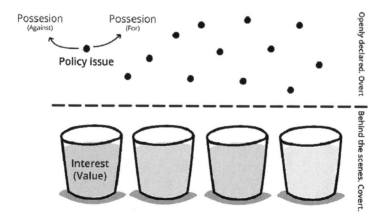

In their classic book on negotiating, *Getting to Yes*, William Yuri and Roger Fisher discuss the difference between a person's "position" and their "interests." A position is mostly about *how* we want to accomplish a desired outcome; most arguments—and even negotiations—revolve around declared positions. Given the fact that, with enough creativity, we can come up with lots of different ways of achieving the same outcome, it is a shame that **positions** hold such substantial weight in arguments while **interests** remain unattended to and even unknown!

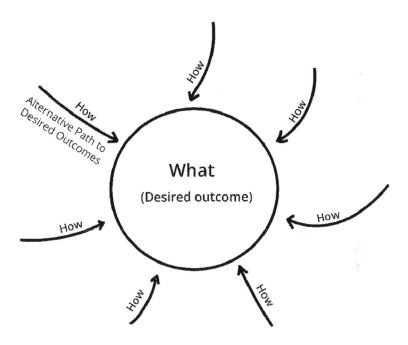

Sparks Are Flying

Katy: "*I can't believe how expensive gas prices are! We need to get a nationwide petition going to lower them. Just think about what it would do for lower income families who struggle to pay for gas and can't afford access to remote employment opportunities. So instead, they get funneled into local jobs, even if these jobs are a bad fit, or simply dead-end jobs. How can they ever break away from their poverty if they can't access better jobs with better pay!?*"

Michael: "*Absolutely not, Katy. We are polluting our environment enough already, thank you very much! We need to stop thinking about making more money and start thinking more about cutting down on pollution.*"

At this point, Katy has two options:

1) She can dive into a direct conflict with Michael, barreling out the gate with a statement like:

   "*Don't you care about people!? Do you know how many poor people we have in our country? Socio-economic gaps are expanding and it's tearing us apart! Not that you would know anything about that, Mr. Upper class Activist.*"

Or...

2) She can delay gratification and spend the next few moments relating to Michael's value system while learning more about where he is coming from:

   "*Yeah, I know—we're polluting our environment like crazy. On one hand, I can't help but feel terrible for the millions of poor people living in our otherwise wealthy country, and on the other hand, I definitely see where you are coming from. No doubt that we are slowly but surely killing our planet.*"

Notice how Katy removes herself from absolute certainly, positioning herself closer to Michael on the "Certainty/Opposing Certainty line" from page?

No, she isn't being fake or manipulative. Instead, she has decided to acknowledge a valid argument against her suggestion. Like it or not, it was a valid argument. Lower gas prices may very well increase driving-related pollution.

And no, this doesn't mean that she's forfeited her suggestion... far from it! Instead, it just shows that she understands the difference between a valid argument and a valid opinion. By not acting on an impulse to tear apart Michael's argument in order to dissolve any threat to her suggestion, she has given Michael reason to see her as both a knowledgeable and moderate person.

Here's something that tends to elude us when we get heated about a particular topic or opinion: *an argument can be valid without automatically invalidating our opinion.* Gas does pollute, that's a fact. Humanity is polluting the planet like crazy, that's also a fact. And yet, in spite of these accurate and troubling facts, poverty does still exist, and lowering gas prices could lower unemployment. While acknowledging the validity of the environmental argument and the legitimacy of Michael's environmental based value system:

a) Katy can still hold the opinion that closing the socioeconomic gap is more important than preventing the added pollution that comes from an increased gas consumption.

b) Katy can try to prove that, by helping lower income families earn more, they can afford higher quality products, which are made of more environmentally safe elements. If she can successfully demonstrate that temporarily increasing gas-related pollution, while permanently reducing consumption-related pollution (due to the exodus of millions from poverty), then Michael can endorse her proposal without having moved an inch from a value-oriented stand point.

Now, you may have noticed that I used the word "if." It may end up, after some research, that Katy may **not** be able to demonstrate a positive correlation between a higher earning capacity and lower consumption-related pollution among poverty-stricken demographics. But had she fallen into the need for absolute certainty gratification trap, this opportunity would have been lost on her. Even after failing to make this correlation, Katy still has yet another option which will allow for the upholding of the Persuasion Equation.

c) She can try to come up with other, less environmentally damaging, ideas of how to enable better access to employment opportunities for low income families. She can suggest free, electricity-powered shuttles from areas with high levels of unemployment that run to adjunct areas with more job opportunities.

The key here is to avoid immediately tagging Michael as "Katy's opponent" and attacking him for not caring about the poor. We need to maintain a clear differentiation between **what** I am trying to achieve and **how** it can be achieved. This gives us an opportunity to be much more flexible and allow Michael's value system to take the lead, provided it does not directly undermine my value system and that my suggestions can be proven to support both of our values (which, contrary to what many people believe, is the case the majority of the time).

And now for the real kicker! Had Katy not even brought up her proposal right away, but rather spent time conversing with Michael on other things, she may have discovered his affinity for the environment. This would have afforded her a new kind of opportunity for introducing her idea in a way that appealed to him right from the start:

> *"I think I may have found a cool way of lowering pollution while also lowering unemployment in poverty stricken areas."*

Or, if she was unable to find data supporting such a link:

> *"I think I may have found a cool transportation solution that can lower unemployment in poverty stricken areas without adding to transportation-related pollution."*

What do you think Michael's most likely, one-word response would be?

"How?"

When you hear this magical word in persuasion-related conversations, you know you are on the right path.

As for Katy, this alternative way of presenting her idea immediately positions her in a more positive way in Michael's mind (and heart!). She cares about the environment and thus is that much closer to him on the Certainty/Opposing Certainty line. This is Katy's reward for taking the time to discover Michael's value system and general interests. In other words, this is Katy's reward for not falling into the false sense of urgency gratification trap and rushing to complain about gas prices.

Michael is not only more likely to support Katy's efforts, but his overall experiential memory of Katy will be extremely positive! In a world as divided as ours, Michael—even if unknowingly—will compare his experience with Katy to the hundreds of interactions where he was quickly attacked and labeled as an "impractical liberal tree hugger."

The most important aspect of this principle is that people don't have to experience the discomfort of having to change their minds in order to be persuaded to support us. In direct continuation of the previous principle (Small Steps), the smallest steps are the ones not taken, as demonstrated by this example.

But what if Katy had kicked off with the suggestion to lower gas prices and triggered Michael's adamant response? Would all be lost? Not at all. While she would be starting at a relative disadvantage compared to some of the examples above, she can still correct her course fairly simply:

Katy: "*So, it's not so much that you don't care about lowering unemployment, but that you instead feel that doing so by lowering the price of gasoline comes at too high a cost from an environmental perspective?*"

Michael: "*That's right.*"

Katy: "*I can definitely respect that! So what if instead of lowering gas prices, we used electric-powered buses to shuttle people from areas with high unemployment to areas*" with richer job opportunities? We can even use electric buses. Also, I think that even if we couldn't use electric buses, the free buses idea can not only lower unemployment and lead to smaller socio-economic gaps in society, but I think it can also prove extremely valuable from an environmental perspective! And that's even in spite of the noise and air pollution that the buses will create."

Michael: "Electric run buses could work… it's certainly better than lowering gas prices nationwide. But how do you see traditional gasoline-powered buses being good for the environment?"

Katy: "Well, the fumes definitely wouldn't be good for the environment, but there is another environmental perspective to consider. If we enabled people living in poverty-stricken areas to access jobs in the city and earn more money, there would be a dramatic change in their daily consumption habits. They could afford better products that were more environmentally friendly, and would have a better opportunity to gain access to education, which is an important factor for an environmentally responsible society."

Michael: "Do you have any statistics that show the link between socio-economic status and environmental responsibility?"

Katy: "Not off the top of my head, but I'm more than happy to look it up! I'll also try to find out if using electric buses is even an option. Who know, I could be a mile off."

Michael: "Cool. You coming to watch the game with us tonight?"

Katy: "You bet!"

As you can see, Katy carefully avoided applying too much pressure and stayed away from trying to force Michael to give up a value that's important to him. As soon as she realized where Michael was coming from, she adapted her approach.

She also avoided the false sense of urgency gratification trap by pausing the conversation. In doing so, and in the way she did ("Let me do some research and get back to you"), she both demonstrated open-mindedness and respect for this value system. More still, Katy also created an opportunity to continue the conversation with Michael at a later time, thus buying herself time to be more prepared when they spoke again. In this way, she was treating persuasion as a process and taking small steps to get to a desired outcome.

But wait - that's not all!

This is where the third gratification trap—our need for credit—roars to life. After all, isn't the sweetest part of a debate when the other person concedes to your superior arguments? I know for me at least, winning has an enticing draw!

In this case, getting credit would likely be Katy's downfall. In the greater scheme of things, why should she care if the environmental value is the tipping point that gets Michael to accept her recommendation? Her strategic goal is to lower unemployment in poverty-stricken areas, **not** bringing down gas prices as it may have first appeared.

And Michael? His strategic goal is a society that is more environmentally responsible. If the electric bus option pans out or, even better, if data is found that proves an increase in monthly income of poor families leads to them having a lower environmental footprint, this not only gives him an opportunity to support the idea without feeling like he's had to compromise on his values. This even allows him the ego-boosting feeling (credit) of driving Katy to a better solution. This is the very essence of this third principle.

Now the question is: "Is there a way to proactively discover the other person's interests and value system?"

There certainly is.

Key Practice #4: Lead with Questions

Leading others to believe they were the ones that found the solution is the antidote to the absolute certainty gratification trap. Not only does it force you into avoiding absolute and far-reaching statements, but it ensures that the other person feels heard.

When teaching how to lead others to our desired conclusions, I like to start with asking people to imagine that they are only allowed to participate in a given conversation by using open-ended questions. This can be extremely frustrating at first. But, when the going gets tough, remind yourself that the person who controls the questions at the base and heart of the discussion effectively controls the conversation and has great influence over its outcome.

So... If your toolbox was limited to questions only, what would they be? *What questions does your position—your point of view—answer?*

Now, just to be clear, not every sentence that ends with a question mark is really a question under the cover of this principle. A "question" that begins with, "Don't you agree that..." or "Isn't it true that..." is not really a question! Instead, it's more like a thinly-veiled answer. Questions like these are known as closed-ended questions. You know that a question is a close-ended one if it can be answered with a simple "yes" or "no." Avoid using these types of questions by opening your questions with the words "What..." or "How..."

Put it into play

Let's say that you want to get someone to agree that the office walls should be painted red. Before flipping to the next page, go ahead and try to structure some open-ended questions that might kick-start a discussion to get you those cherry-colored walls you have your fingers crossed for!

(No cheating! Think of a few questions before turning the page. Go ahead and write them down.)

1._____

2._____

3._____

4._____

5._____

Now, how many of the questions you came up with contain the word red?

Couldn't help yourself, could you?

Know why?

More than likely, it is because you were focused more on your own point of view than on that of the person you are trying to persuade. You were busy trying to structure questions that would lead the other person to the conclusion—your conclusion—that red is the best choice. This approach stems first and foremost from a latent sense of urgency and also from a strong sense of certainty. There's a better way to go about this.

Instead of "leading the witness," you should have tried to structure questions that will help you to understand where they are coming from (remember Katy and Michael?).

You were in a "!" state of mind. Maybe you were incredibly excited about the possibility of red walls and let it drive your thinking, but as we have already seen, this enthusiasm could unintentionally work against you.

What you need is to be in a "?" state of mind. Turn your excitement into curiosity for whatever it is the other person is thinking. Allow discovering their desires to be an integral part of your persuasion strategy. Think about it as the preliminary reconnaissance in your mission to recruit this person.

And, for those of you that were able to compose questions without slipping in the word "red," good job! It can be extremely tough to take a step back and allow others to shine.

In order to use questions effectively, you have to temporarily set aside your own point of view and *become truly curious about how the other person sees the world.* The more you know about—and understand—where the other person is coming from and where they are aiming to get to, the more likely you are to be able to carve out a path that connects them to your point of view. Or rather, that connects your point of view to them.

The question now is, "What is the best way to use open ended questions and what should my questions be focused on?"

Key Practice #5: Talk to people about themselves and they will listen to you for *hours*!

This Dale Carnegie quote is one of my favorites. Think about each of the gratification traps we have discussed so far. What do they all have in common?

They are *all about us.* **We** need to feel gratified, and the sooner it happens, the better.

The destructive power of these traps is derived from the very reasons that we normally engage in debates: *we* have an opinion that *we* are passionate about, and that *we* want to spread as far and often as possible.

You better believe that technology has only compounded this mindset. As I have already mentioned earlier in this book, while technological evolution has given us remarkable communication outlets and reach, and while social networks allow us to broadcast our lives 24/7, it is harder than ever to get people's attention. In the 21st century, it is this reality that continues to feed gratification traps. The harder it is to get attention, the harder we fall into them.

And yet, this modern day attention scarcity offers us a powerful, albeit counterintuitive, opportunity to shine bright. If people are starved for attention… let's give it to them.

If you want to get someone's attention and ultimately persuade them over to your way of thinking, you will need to hand them swathes of your attention. This is exactly what the fourth and fifth principles are all about (leading with questions that focus on their origins and desires).

The more attention you give someone, the more they will want to engage with you. And, of course, the more they want to engage with you, the more opportunities you will have to influence them. After all, persuasion is a process!

Give them the spotlight

To avoid all three gratification traps and push yourself to become a master persuader, you have to try—even if just temporarily—to put the person you are communicating with at the center of your attention. Momentarily set aside your own agenda and **give them the spotlight.**

Start by limiting your participation to asking open-ended questions. Make sure that these questions are all about *them*.

Rather than focusing on coming up with the most intelligent or foolproof arguments, or dedicating all of your fantastic brainpower to finding weaknesses or loopholes in their approach, focus on understanding their point of view:

- What seems to be its origin?
- Where are they coming from?

- What core values are at the base of their belief?
- What is driving them?
- What do they hope to achieve?
- Who are they as a person?
- What other areas of their lives does it link to?

When leading with questions, follow up is the key. Let each answer they give lead way to a follow-up question. Make it your mission to know as much about them as possible, using each question to leapfrog your way to new answers.

And remember... there is no urgency! Embrace persuasion as a process. You're in no real rush. And if you are in a rush, this is even more crucial. Slower will get you there faster.

The Subtlest War

Bruce: "*Can you believe that they're even considering pulling back the troops from Iraq?*"

Josh: "*I take it that you are opposed to that...*"

Bruce: "*Absolutely! If we withdraw now, the last decade will have been for nothing. Not to mention that the entire country will become a major hub for terrorism.*"

Josh: "*What do you think our country's course of action should be regarding Iraq and global terrorism?*"

Bruce: "*We need to keep our troops on the ground for one. We also have to start kicking some major ass over there and send those terrorist nutcases a very clear message—we won't be messed with. That's the only thing they understand, and believe me it's the only approach they actually respect.*"

Josh: "*What do you mean by 'kick some ass?' What do you think we should do?*"

Bruce: "*Air bomb the hell out of them. None of this 'we don't want to hurt innocent civilians' crap. Start shooting indiscriminately and they will quickly understand that hiding behind civilians is no longer effective.*"

Josh: "*Just air bombs? Is that enough to win?*"

Bruce: "*No, that's just for starters. We need more boots on the ground. Take back all the ground those crazies managed to capture and keep pushing them until they have nowhere left to run.*"

Josh: "*How many more soldiers will that require?*"

Bruce: "*As many as it takes. That's what we have a military for, right? Look, as soon as you start slowing down and showing weakness, they get even bolder. That's what we're seeing now... I mean they're beheading people!*"

Josh: "*Yeah, I know. It's crazy, sometimes I can't believe the cruelty. How people can do such things is beyond me.*"

Bruce: "*Exactly! That's why we have to stop them.*"

Josh: "*How long do you think our forces would need to be there? Do you think they'll have to stay there permanently?*"

Bruce: "*Hard to say. I think they need to stay there for as long as it takes. I guess for at least a few years... that's for sure!*"

Josh: "*Hmm... I wouldn't want to be a soldier over there. Do you have friends in the military?*"

Bruce: "*Not any more. A friend of mine served for a few years though. Man, did he have some stories!*"

Josh: "*Really? Two of my friends also served...*"

Bruce: "*You don't say! When? What unit were they in?*"

As you can see, this example could have easily gone on for quite a few more pages. Did you notice the difference between the absolute, even troubling at times, nature of Bruce's statements against the open-ended type of questions by Josh? Despite whatever he might have been thinking, Josh didn't express any opinion in the matter. Instead, he related in the ways that he could, and it has nothing to do with their positions on this matter. Bruce could have represented a completely opposite belief with just as much troubling certainty, and Josh would have been equally wise to lead the conversation with open-ended question.

Notice how the conversation progresses and eventually makes its way to his friend's experiences in the military? Normally, if you were to disagree with Bruce's opening remarks, your first response might be one that challenges the statement and immediately offers an opposing point of view.

We've all been there and done that. What you're likely looking at is a swift escalation in tone and attitude; things are about to get heated. But, by leading with questions and not rushing into a full-on argument, Josh is able to learn more about Bruce and his way of thinking. The overall result—a much more pleasant conversation and the discovery of some common denominators between them. So now Bruce can frame Josh in his mind as someone he has something in common with, rather than someone who has opposing views. Now Josh can use cognitive dissonance to his advantage. You see, if Bruce formulates a positive impression of Josh early on, then the universal human desire not to change will work in favor of Josh if and when he says or does something Bruce doesn't approve of (how many times have you demonstrated greater leniency towards someone you like versus someone you didn't know or didn't like?).

Now this isn't to say that Josh's approach will ultimately lead Bruce to abandon his beliefs and become a "bleeding-heart," antiwar liberal. But during this conversation, Bruce might start to be more open to adopting certain exceptions to his statements, "Don't worry about protecting innocent civilians" and "Our troops should stay there as long as needed." We can also expect that he will be more tolerant, even if just slightly, of an alternative view when Josh finally decides to share it.

There are many benefits to engaging in this way, especially in the earlier stages of the persuasion process:

- **Avoiding the gratification traps**

  When I first introduced the three gratification traps, my key objective was to raise your awareness of them. It's harder to avoid what you can't see. It's so darn easy to fall into them, that the first step is simply to understand that they exist and to know what they look like.

- **Gain valuable information**

  As we have seen, persuasion is a whole lot more than rational arguments and supporting data. Persuasion requires you to know as much about the person you are trying to persuade as you do about the topic you are discussing. The more that you know and understand about them, the better use you can make of the knowledge you have about the matter at hand.

- **Meta-persuasion**

  Being a truly effective persuader is about adopting the long game. It's about understanding that the nature of your conversation on Monday will have a powerful impact on the other person's outlook and willingness to engage with you on Thursday (even about a completely different topic).

It's not always about what you say. But it is always about how others feel when they interact with you. Do they enjoy these interactions, or are they a pain? How people remember feeling around you will determine much of your ability to persuade them, regardless of the topic at hand. And, given that they too are starved for attention and have the same unrelenting need for instant gratification, the door is open for you to become the person that gives them much-valued conversational gratifications. The result will be a positive experiential memory of you and a stronger predisposition to engage with you, listen to and respect your opinions, and ultimately support your efforts, whatever they may be. And that is what lasting impact looks like.

Wrapping things up

Each of these five principles have something in common—they will be incredibly difficult to apply from the start. Each and every one of them is counter-intuitive to what nature and society teach us, and they all require us to abandon bad habits that have been formed over a lifetime. But you can do it. You now have powerful tools at your disposal, and you can train your persuasion muscles by putting these practices into play! Combined, all five principles create a perpetually self-reinforcing momentum that propels you forward:

1. If you have a longer process...

2. You can afford to use smaller steps. Smaller steps lower the chances of triggering cognitive dissonance and therefore generate less resistance.

3. The smallest—and most influential—step is leveraging pre-existing conclusions they have already reached in support of your opinions and proposals.

4. The best way to get others to reach their own conclusions is by leading them with open-ended questions.

5. Ask questions about them. Not in a challenging way (no cross-examinations!), but in a sincerely curious way. The more you talk about *them*, the more they will want to talk with *you*. There's your process!

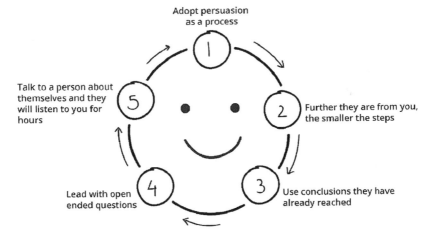

And, if ever in doubt, remind yourself to always ensure that:

Engaging with you = Positive experiential memory

Now go out and change the world!

-Ariel Halevi

www.vayomar.com

Give yourself some down time

N ow that you've learned how to "turn on" your persuasion skills, I like to speak for a moment about the importance of knowing how to turn them off.

Delaying gratification can be draining. I know that even today, after so many years of practice, I still walk away from certain conversations feeling depleted. It's called "will power" for a good reason. Not reaching for that marshmallow can eat up our battery power and when our battery is depleted, we can make some serious mistakes.

That's why it's very important to be aware of your own predisposition. Pay attention to your own tendencies when it comes to having impulses and with regards to how hard it is for your to apply delayed gratification. Like when we first go to the gym, we need to gradually build up our muscles and not rush in and try to lift the heaviest weights right from the start. And even if you have been going to the gym for years, as I have in the context of persuasion, you need to listen to your body and manage yourself accordingly.

That's why I have adopted a policy of allocating time to free fall into gratification traps. Sometimes it can be when i'm Facebook debating with friends, and other times around the family dinner table or with close friends. I let myself go and bubble up several marshmallows at a time. I do it knowing that I will not have meaningful impact in those specific interactions and that's ok.

I do it to have fun. To enjoy myself.

I know that these people, who are close to me, know me and love me enough to take it and that it will not significantly compromise my "Messenger Status" with them due to our long standing relationships. I also do it around topics that are less critical to me. I do it to built up my energy for those tougher, more important conversations with people with whom I may not have the same strong relationship foundations and in which I will need every ounce of self control and discipline in order to avoid the gratification traps and really have a chance at lasting impact with them.

Our energy to deal with the world around us is a resource like any other. It can be spent and we can run low. When this happens, we are at a greater risk of damaging potentially important relationships and setting ourselves back, sometimes way back.

That's why it's important for me to make sure you work hard, but also responsibly, at learning how to use the tools I have presented in this book. Take your time doing this. Don't rush it and don't over do it. Move slow and steady and be conscious of the emotional affect it's having on you. Don't be too tough on yourself and let yourself enjoy that first marshmallow every now and again.

Remember: slow is not necessarily slower.

Thank you

I have wanted to write a book for a long time. I must have written four that I ended up not publishing. Verbal communication is quite different than written communication and I realized that I needed lots of help. I am so grateful that I am fortunate enough to have had many people make sure I got it. Most especially, **Doug Crowe**. One of the wonderful outcomes of this book, even before it has been published, was discovering you. In so many ways, you made this book a reality, where once it was only a dream for me. I know few people who can balance, so perfectly, such a high level of expertise with such endless patience and good nature. I enjoyed every moment of this process with you and can't wait to start working with you on the next book!

Gur Braslavi. My business partner of 15 years and the brother I never had. As with many accomplishments I look back on with joy, this too, is one I know was made possible by your unwavering love and support. You are a remarkable person and a role model for me. Thanks for existing!

My family. Having a a great mentor, especially early in life is a tremendous privilege. I was remarkably lucky to have two incredible mentors from as early as I can remember: my father, Menashe who laid the foundations of my analytical thinking when he taught me chess at the age of 5 and continued training throughout my life, until he passed away in 1999 and my mother Esther who introduced me to the world of organizational consulting and coaching back when I was still in middle school. Ema - you are still my number one mentor and I count my blessings for having you both as my parents. And the same goes to you, my amazing sister, Naama, Dana and Sigal. We don't pick our families and I sure lucked out!

Made in the USA
Lexington, KY
04 September 2018